ONE
SMALL
WORD

ONE SMALL WORD

Surviving childhood abuse

Gloria Eveleigh

urlink
PRINT & MEDIA

1603 Capitol Ave., Suite 310 Cheyenne, Wyoming USA 82001
1-888-980-6523 | admin@urlinkpublishing.com

URLink Publishing is committed to excellence in the publishing industry.

Book design copyright © 2018 by URLink Publishing. All rights reserved.

Published in the United States of America
ISBN 978-1-64367-158-1 (Paperback)
ISBN 978-1-64367-160-4 (Digital)

1. Genre1
2. Genre2
13.12.18

DEDICATION

I am dedicating this book to my big sister who has always blamed herself for not protecting us younger siblings from our father's abuse. I want you to know, Sandra, it was not your fault in any way, and I'll always love you for what you went through for our sake.

Acnowledgements

My grateful and heartfelt thanks go to:

Joanie and John Wood, retired probation officer working with perpetrators, and retired child protection social worker working with victims, who loyally provided encouragement, feedback and editing throughout the writing process, and who have become valued friends as a result.

The Author Learning Centre and all those experts who delivered the webinars on its Book in a Year Course that gave me the tools I needed to write my first novel. Not forgetting Pamela Joy, Mary Mangee, Renee Weldon and Dennis Shaeffer, all members of my author circle who gave me advice, encouragement & feedback that helped me reach the end of my book.

Bob Tart, a published author, who I met on an authors' chat line, and who gave me an invaluable kick-start with my first chapter.

Ann Pither and Marion Johnson, both supportive and close friends; Geoff Patmore, a long-term friend and work colleague who always believed in me; and Kathy Schilbach, Sean Clark, Lee Cowan, and June Sullivan, all members of my community, who contributed in different ways to me reaching the end of the writing process.

Members of my family including India, my lovely 18-year-old granddaughter, who provided feedback, encouragement, love, and a total belief in me; Sandra, Geoff and Jackie, my siblings, who were and still are there for me in both bad and good times; and my son and daughter-in-law Chris and Emma, whose support and unconditional love have helped me get through.

Kevin Long of Kevin and Rae Photograpy, who miraculously produced my author photo despite me being camera shy.

Geri Burnikell, Co-ordinator of 'Support Line', the organisation for victims of historical child abuse, who kindly wrote the foreword for this book.

Last but not least, Janet Doyle, my professional editor who transformed my rough diamond into a polished gem, and to whom I will be forever grateful.

Foreword

ONE SMALL WORD - SURVIVING CHILDHOOD ABUSE

As Co-ordinator of a charity, which has supported survivors of child abuse for many years, I was delighted to be asked to write the foreword to this book which takes us on a journey with Frankie, a mature social work student, who was abused both physically and sexually at home for many years in her childhood.

As with many survivors Frankie had underestimated the massive impact that her abuse would have in later life and it was as a mature social work student that she was triggered when working with a family in which abuse was disclosed. Being in the presence of the perpetrator brought back to Frankie memories of her father abusing her and all the feelings of anger and hate towards him and the shame and guilt she felt as a child.

The reader is given a very vivid understanding of the very sad childhood which Frankie led, although with some glimpses of normality and happiness such as family Christmases and enjoyable times spent with grandparents. Much of Frankie's childhood was based on fear, desperately trying, along with her siblings, to escape the clutches of her volatile and violent father while for many years enduring the most horrific sexual abuse.

———

We hear of the desperate loneliness Frankie felt as a child, her feelings of despair and the lack of love she was shown by her parents. We are given an insight into Frankie's life as an adult, the marriage she felt pressured into, the affairs she had, the births of her children, family life and all her soul searching and heartache along the way which were interspersed with happier times.

We see how through the counselling process Frankie came to have a deeper understanding of how the abuse had affected her life and behaviour as an adult. She saw how not having the respect of her father as a child or the respect of her mother who colluded with the abuse, had led to her having no respect for herself. Having very much been at the control of others in her childhood she understood how as an adult she had succumbed to the control of others. Frankie had very low self esteem, and did not believe she was worthy of being liked or loved, had difficulty in expressing love and how to respond to men appropriately. Frankie shares with us her tremendous guilt and shame over what happened and how the abuse had robbed her of her childhood and innocence.

Counselling helped Frankie to see the feelings she had were perfectly normal, that the abuse was not her fault, it was ok to like herself, she was worthy of love, and that the responsibility for the abuse belonged to the perpetrator, and not on her shoulders.

Through our work with survivors we know that many suffer in silence, some for many years, often the shame and guilt preventing them from seeking help. The counselling showed what a difference reaching out to others can make and led to Frankie being free of her thoughts, which had haunted her for over forty years. Frankie's counsellor had said to her that what you learn as a child is really hard to unlearn in adulthood and that is so very true. This is often why survivors have so many difficulties and struggles in adult years where they often carry around the burden of the feelings and thoughts they were made to feel as a child.

I feel that when survivors speak out about their own abuse it is a great help to others struggling to make some kind of sense of the way they feel. This book very much shows how, with support and a greater understanding and awareness, that it is possible to make changes to one's beliefs which have been held for many years. It is an inspiration to those with their own struggles as Frankie showed through her determination, her strength, her courage, and her resilience, how to turn negative experiences into positive ones. To gain some semblance of healing from the trauma of abuse is often a long and painful journey but Frankie shows us that much can be attained and achieved and how her own experiences enabled her to empathise with and help others in the career that she had chosen. The book inspires the reader never to give up hope as it is possible to reach a stage in life where the past does not adversely affect one's daily life and one can attain a sense of normality, peace and happiness. I would thoroughly recommend this book to all those who have been affected by the impact of child abuse on their lives and to those who work with survivors as a source of hope and inspiration and the importance of seeking help and support from others and breaking the silence which surrounds abuse.

Geri Burnikell
Co-ordinator
SupportLine
Reg. charity 1097419

—1—

It'll come back and hit you

Frankie – aged 50

"I really wanted to slowly strangle that old man, strangle him until his eyes popped out," says Frankie, with tears running down her cheeks.

Her manager looks mildly alarmed, as well she might. It's not the sort of thing a mature social work student should be saying about a client's husband. Frankie knows she is acting more like a fifteen-year-old than an adult of fifty, but she has just had the worst experience of her adult life and is trying to make sense of it.

"You know you'll need to sort this out before you can continue with your career, don't you?" says her manager gently as she hands Frankie the box of tissues from the corner of her desk.

Frankie is still trembling. Not exactly appropriate behaviour in the learning disabilities team. Her placement had been going well, and now this! She is embarrassed but still can't stop the tears.

"I truly wanted to see him struggle for breath until he could breath no more," she continues. "The old pervert had caused such fear and pain. I know it was years ago, but I wanted him to know what was happening, to experience some of what he had done."

The manager looks across the desk. Her large, kind eyes travel over Frankie's face. She doesn't comment about the smears on Frankie's glasses, or the tracks of mascara snaking down her cheeks.

"What happened?" she asks.

And so Frankie tells the woman across the desk, the woman who had once complimented Frankie on her kryptonite bottom, what had just happened.

The old man's wife was the team's client. She had a fairly significant learning disability, discovered when the police referred her to social services. Frankie's role was to put in place safeguards against further violence from the husband who she refused to leave.

For the last two months Frankie had been providing support to this woman, and had managed to ignore the frail elderly gentleman who was apparently capable of punching his wife. No problem. But then one of his daughters rang and let slip that he'd sexually abused her and her sister when they were children. Frankie had updated the file notes, reported the information to her supervisor and carried on as usual. She had heard it before, quite often. And she knew what it meant for sure, because she had been there too. Frankie's own experience of abuse seemed to make her a magnet for those whose childhoods had also been shattered. All okay. Until today. Thirty minutes ago she had to force herself to leave that old man's house and his too submissive wife before she put her hands around his throat and squeezed hard.

She'd made it to the car before she started to shake. Frankie hadn't been all that surprised at the daughter's disclosure, because her sixth sense had been twitching every time she saw the old man. And, after all, dealing with this sort of thing was what she wanted to do, help people. Leaving a perfectly good job as a research scientist in order to retrain in social work had not been a difficult decision. But where did this rage come from?

The wife was not home on this visit. Frankie had sat in the dining room, sun streaming in the window, chatting quite amiably with the old man, when it started. Her heart began to race, and suddenly she knew she wanted to kill him. It wasn't just that he was the first actual perpetrator she had to work with; he had suddenly morphed into a vision of her father. She blinked, but it was still her father sitting there, not some frail yet violent old man wearing faded brown corduroy trousers. She breathed deeply, stood up, and took her murderous thoughts out the front door.

"Sorry, I must go. I forgot an urgent appointment," was all she could manage.

She calmed down a bit more in the car, but by the time she had driven to the office and sat herself in front of the manager she had lost it again.

"Here, have another tissue," Her manager says.

Frankie sniffs and wipes away her tears.

"How about some counselling on this? It's obviously really hit a nerve."

Frankie can only nod. She knows this day has hit her like a sledgehammer, and she knows where it has come from.

Once home, she picks up the telephone and asks the doctor's receptionist for an appointment. Before the day is out her doctor has organised six sessions of 'Talking Therapy', which will commence in five weeks' time. That, and the fact that her manager has taken her off the case, means that it is possible life will return to normal.

Five weeks later she is shaking hands with the counsellor. They meet at the local hospital. The counsellor is a tall, slim, well-dressed woman in her mid forties. She has a calm aura about her, which helps put Frankie at ease. They have one hour to explore her uncharacteristic reaction.

"I'm not usually the violent type," Frankie begins, "that's what's shocked me the most. I'm on my second marriage, have managed successfully to bring up three children without them having suffered any significant mental or physical damage, and I've even been able to protect three cats, a guinea pig and a silver miniature rabbit to the point where all but the rabbit died of natural causes."

"What happened to the rabbit?"

"Oh, for some unknown reason, he kept thumping so hard on the floor of his cage that he broke his back and had to be put down." Frankie realises she is grinning despite the story being slightly gruesome.

"And three children?"

"Yes, twenty-seven, twenty-three, and sixteen, now."

"So, tell me what happened to you."

After a couple of minutes, Frankie starts talking.

"I think the telephone call from my client's daughter hit me harder than I realised," she says.

"Why do you think that was?" the counsellor asks.

"He died before I could get back at him."

'Who?"

"My father. Deep down I have a real need to inflict physical injury on my dad for what he did to me," Frankie confesses hesitantly, "but he died before I could do it, and I'm really, really *angry* that he got away with it."

Frankie is stunned and relieved at the same time. As the words came out of her mouth she recognised them as true. This is the first time she has really understood, admitted to herself how she feels, and here she is sharing her innermost thoughts with a stranger. The past lifts from her slight shoulders, and she feels lighter.

"Did that help? Did saying that help? Is there anything else?"

"I don't know and I'm frightened that if I look into that part of my brain, I might find memories that are even worse than the ones I've dealt with," Frankie says. Then she adds, "... and I'm not sure I'm ready for that."

They talk more about Frankie's family and her placement with the learning disabilities team. Then the counsellor looks up at the clock.

"During the coming week, I'd like you to think over what we've discovered today to see if anything else emerges," says the counsellor, "next week we can explore any new memories that come to mind."

Frankie is stunned that the whole hour has gone. She comes away feeling drained. She is still surprised at what she has just said. Surely she has already dealt with all her bad experiences. She is definitely not going to do any more thinking about the incident this coming week. She has put the opener to a can of worms today, and if she thought about any more things right now, the contents of that can might eat her alive.

During the week, she tries to put the whole counselling session to the back of her mind. However, a new memory does come to the surface and she finds herself wrestling with it, especially in her dreams at night. She has a very unsettled seven days. She's so distracted that it's hard to concentrate at work. She struggles to make any progress with her other cases, and finds herself counting the days until her next counselling appointment finally arrives.

This time her handshake with the counsellor is a little more apprehensive. She feels sure the woman senses how she's feeling as she does her best to put Frankie at ease with small talk about the weather. At least she doesn't ask anymore about the rabbit. It takes only a few minutes for Frankie to settle under the woman's calm aura.

"She's good!" Frankie thinks to herself.

And then the counsellor asks the question Frankie's been waiting for.

— 2 —

Frankie's memory -
A painful awakening

Frankie – aged 15

"Frankie, go and make us a cup of tea!"

Frankie's father, Frederick, has always been a dominant, arrogant and portly man. His stomach juts at the world. His dark hair and moustache sit on him as if they landed there in a bad mood.

Frankie hears him through the fog of half sleep. The words hang there but she is too relaxed to do anything about them.

"Frankie, tea now!" her father repeats. She stays warm and where she is. She squints at the clock. It is only seven o'clock and it's Sunday morning. Surely she doesn't have to get up yet. It's been a hard slog all week studying for her GCEs. She returns to dreaming about last night and her first real date. The hated voice can wait; the voice that has become darker and more full of temper ever since she finally managed to say 'no' to what had been going on since before she was three years old.

She knows it's risky, but she snuggles back down into the double bed she inherited from her beautiful 18-year-old sister, Patricia. Since Patricia married Anton several months ago Frankie has enjoyed Patricia's bed and her pretty kidney-shaped dressing table with its adjustable mirrors and flouncy, pink floral drapes that hide the drawers beneath. Frankie's precious miniature glass animals graze in two bright translucent herds on the glass top. The jewellery box her grandmother gave her on her thirteenth birthday sits there too, growing purple rose buds on its lid. She is starting to think about last night again when the bedroom door flies open to reveal the beast. In that split second her world and her heart seem to close down.

His hand speeds towards her face and before she feels the blow on her cheek she knows he's erupted again. It always makes him stink more. His face, when she opens her eyes, is that horrible red colour. She's pushed her luck too far. He hits again; this time it's her ear and the ringing is immediate. She clings to the soft armour of the bed covers and pulls them up over her head.

"I told you to get up and make your mother and me a cup of tea!" he shouts at the top of his voice. She lets out a small shriek as her father wrenches the sheets away and throws them to the floor. She rolls away and tangles herself in her nightdress. He hits again, and pulls her towards him by the hem of that garment. Her flaying arms and legs are no defence. Her panic climbs like a tsunami and she hears her own pleading voice. "Stop, stop, please, please, stop!" The bile rises to her mouth. 'I'm going to die,' she thinks, curling up like a hedgehog without spines. The blows keep coming and she doesn't care anymore. The final punch to her shoulder makes pain shoot everywhere and she sobs.

Then, cursing the day she was born, he sweeps all her bright glass animals to the floor and storms out of the room, slamming the door on his trembling daughter. The door opens again.

"Now get down those stairs and make that tea right now!"

Frankie gets to her feet, and hobbles downstairs to the kitchen, completely forgetting that her little sister Janet must have observed the whole episode from her top bunk at the other end of the bedroom.

When she gets upstairs again Janet is hiding under her bed covers, pale and trembling. There are tears of panic trying to struggle out of her tightly screwed up six-year-old eyes. Frankie guides her down the steps from her top bunk and without one word leads her towards her own double bed where not so long ago she had been enjoying her early morning dreams. She slides under the covers and pulls Janet in next to her. Their tears mingle to form an expanding wet patch on the pillow.

— 3 —

A journey back in time

Frankie – aged 50

As Frankie finishes describing her memory of thirty-five years ago, she notices tears in the corner of the counsellor's eyes. Not until the woman takes a tissue out of a box on a small table next to her chair and hands it to Frankie, does she realise that tears are streaming down her own face. She is very embarrassed. She seems to have spent both of her counselling sessions crying. Her cheeks blush bright red as she apologises.

"No need," says the counsellor, dabbing at her own eyes.

It comforts Frankie to know that this woman is able to feel her feelings with her. Her warmth seems to encompass Frankie's whole being. She breathes a deep sigh of relief and gratitude for this kind soul who is with her all the way. The counsellor's next question surprises her.

"Can you tell me a little more about Janet?" she asks.

Frankie takes her usual couple of minutes thinking time before she attempts to answer the question.

"Well, I know that Janet heard our father curse the day that I was born. And she, like me, felt unwanted." Frankie and Janet had discussed this on several occasions as adults. "My parents only ever wanted two children, a girl and a boy. So really, Patricia and William were all they wanted. I wasn't really necessary and Janet was an accident. In fact she was lucky to have survived after our mother, Joanna, apparently threw herself down the stairs when she was pregnant with Janet, hoping to lose the baby. But it turned out it was twins, a boy and a girl, and the boy was lost."

"Mmmmm. Now I know a bit about how Janet fits in. Was your relationship with her affected, do you think, because of seeing all that happen to you?"

"It made us closer, stronger together. We knew we would always somehow protect each other. When she grew up we became inseparable. And then, much later she told me that Dad had molested her too. She was afraid to tell even me back then, in case he started beating her too. Even at six years of age she knew she'd better do what he wanted."

"She told you about sexual abuse?"

"Yes. He was doing it to her too, the pervert. I didn't find out until she was twenty-three, and I was married with a child. So, you see, we weren't able to protect each other after all. It was horrible when I found that out."

"And Patricia?"

"Yes. Her too. She was really upset when she discovered all three of us had been abused. She always thought that by giving in to Dad, she was protecting us. It hit her hard when she found out that her strategy had failed."

"Where was your brother throughout all of this?"

"William? We knew Dad hit William but Patricia, Janet and I think our bloody uncle, Dad's brother, James, abused him. Uncle James used to stay over and share William's box room, even though it was so small, and only one bed in it. James was supposed to sleep on the box platform, but we don't think he did. William would wet the bed when Uncle James stayed overnight."

"Have you ever asked your brother about it?"

"Yes but he just says that our uncle was a great guy who provided him with the attention that he didn't get from Dad."

Frankie and the counsellor both glance at the clock on the wall.

"Our time is up, Frankie. You look tired."

Frankie does indeed feel quite drained, wrung out.

"I hope talking about the others made you less afraid about delving into your past. We'll carry on next week."

Frankie leaves the hospital in a daze of exhaustion.

Some new memories emerge in the following days. More beatings, unspoken worry about Janet, the time she banged her head when he shoved her. She tries to apply fairness. Maybe Dad and Uncle James had suffered some of the same, and were only kind of passing all that horribleness on. She reminds herself that there must have been some good times in her childhood, but right now she can't remember any at all.

— 4 —

Happy Christmas

Frankie – aged 4

"Wake up, wake up! Santa's been."

Frankie feels her young brother William shaking her roughly. She opens her eyes to see his bright red, two-year old hair at her eye level, before he disappears back down the wooden ladder from her top bunk bed. She peers over the edge to see him sitting on the rug next to their big sister, Patricia, who is still asleep in the bunk below. He is clinging with trembling hands to his precious Christmas delivery. When he looks up at Frankie even the freckles on his nose look happy.

Frankie looks over to the door and sees the strip of yellow light shining brightly through the gap at the bottom. That means her parents are up, so kids are allowed up too. She leans over and shakes Patricia awake. Patricia leaps up, grabs the bulging pillowcase from the end of her bunk and returns to the warmth of the bedclothes. Frankie climbs down with her own pillowcase and slips beneath Patricia's covers. William is not even shivering in the cold morning air. He has already torn the wrapping off one present.

Frankie and Patricia begin their annual ritual. They simultaneously dip their hands into the intriguing contents of their pillowcases. They remove one parcel each and carefully proceed to press, poke and feel it, trying to guess what's inside, with thoughtful expressions on their faces. Then Frankie says, "Oldest first."

The sound of the vacuum cleaner creeps under the door as they unwrap their presents. Their mother vacuums every morning at six o'clock. The whirring of her favourite tool is not going to be silenced just because it's Christmas Day.

"I got a Thooty!" exclaims William. He sticks his hand inside the bright yellow furry Sooty puppet.

"Make it clap," Frankie tells William.

"I have a Sweep puppet!" cries Patricia.

William and Patricia make their puppets fight each other. Patricia is good at playing puppets and William is delighted. Sooty and Sweep are really going at it.

Frankie presses and feels each of her unopened presents before selecting one that is mostly soft to the feel but has a hard lump at one end. She hopes this will be a hand puppet too. She tears away the wrapping and shouts excitedly, "And I have a Sue!"

Soon Frankie's black and white furry puppet is in the middle of a play fight with Sooty and Sweep, but William objects.

"Thue can't fight. She kind."

"Oh yes, she can," says Frankie.

"Thooty's the best so he hath to win!" says William as he gives the Sue and Sweep puppets a furry shove. The girls laugh.

"Let's open some more presents, Frankie," says Patricia.

When Frankie unwraps her next parcel she screws the coloured paper into a ball and throws it at Patricia. William thinks this is a great idea so he copies her, and when Patricia feels the need to defend herself a paper snowball fight fills the room with bright coloured squeals.

Later Patricia gathers up the paper balls, because she is a tidy girl and the eldest. Patricia is always looking after things. She can be a bit bossy at times, Frankie thinks, but that's all right because she is beautiful, with her straight hair and her brown eyes. Frankie has pale blue-grey eyes and they are not nearly as nice as Patricia's, especially the one that squints. Even Frankie's glasses can't make her eyes nice like Patricia's. At the hospital they always tell Frankie that her eyes are lovely, but then they make her do stupid exercises. And Frankie wishes her hair were straight like Patricia's, not all curly and wiggly. At least it's not red like William's.

"Let's go downstairs and see if there is anything more under the tree," says Patricia.

It is black in the hallway, but Patricia leads the way, holding William and Frankie's hands. They feel their way to the lounge door. When they go in they see the tree is twinkling in the corner. The coal fire is still burning, light rolling behind its small brown doors. At the bottom of the tree there are *lots* of large, colourfully wrapped parcels. Frankie lets out a cheer, William squeaks, and Patricia grins. Then their parents open the lounge door and shout at them. But this time it is only "Happy Christmas!"

The children all take their turn to hug Mummy and Daddy. Then it's "Into the kitchen for breakfast. Hurry up." They all follow Joanna towards the first special food of the day.

Frankie sits next to her father at the scrubbed wooden table. He seems in a good mood. William and Patricia are on the other side. Their mother lifts the enormous iron frying pan to the heat and puts the bacon on to sizzle. Soon there are also eggs and fried bread sputtering. Joanna is a skinny mother but she can cook eggs and bacon really well.

It smells so good that Frankie wants to hug her, but knows she wouldn't be allowed to hug while her mother is cooking.

The day continues to be really good. After breakfast they wash their hands and faces in the bathroom and go upstairs to get properly dressed. They must look good for the rest of the family. Patricia has a white organza dress with pink embroidered rosebuds at the hem. Frankie helps her do up the small pink rosebud-shaped buttons down the back, and tie the pink sashes into a large bow. William wriggles while Patricia helps him into his liberty bodice and cream-coloured soft shirt. She buttons his shirt to his shorts and slips a little brown bow tie to his collar. He gets into his slippers and heads downstairs.

Although Frankie wishes she had a proper new dress she really likes her outfit. It used to be Patricia's so it's a bit big, but it's got puff sleeves and a white lace collar and it's red velvet. Patricia ties the bow at Frankie's back.

Downstairs Frederick drags extra chairs into the lounge for the guests, and soon Nan and Granddad arrive. That's probably the best part really. Nan and Granddad sit just near the door and it feels just as good as when Frankie gets to see them on the weekends sometimes. Aunty Dilys and Uncle Bob wink and smile at Frankie. Penny and Paula, Aunty Dilys's girls, are there too. Frankie's Godmother, Aunty Orla, and her husband, Uncle Dan, sit nearest to the Christmas tree, which seems a bit unfair because they might get to choose which presents to open first and Frankie wants to do that.

Frankie doesn't really like the fizzy orange drink that her dad hands her because fizzy bubbles hurt her nose, but she must have it because it's Christmas. Daddy is flirting with Aunty Orla, and all the adults are sipping sherry, which is probably worse stuff than fizzy orange. Maybe she should go into the kitchen and tell her mother about Aunty Orla and

Daddy, but maybe she should not. She waits and sniffs the smell of the turkey cooking.

That day everyone sits around on all the chairs they can find, including the ones from the garden, and Joanna puts everything on the middle of the table. Sherry is followed by cool white wine. Turkey juices run down Aunty Orla's chin, and the stuffing is really good. There is even an extra potato for Frankie. And it is lovely sitting quiet while everyone makes scraping noises on their plates with their knives and forks. The cracker jokes are even mostly funny. Daddy's face gets a bit red, and so does Granddad's. Daddy bangs on the table, sploshes the brandy and makes the pudding burst into flames. Then everyone stands up to say something about the Queen. After that the guests sort of go to sleep, except for the kids who play snakes and ladders for a while. Later, Frankie has to hand around the biscuits but she doesn't get to have the gold-covered one she wanted. Then kids are allowed to open the presents. Frankie gets a flat cardboard doll that you have to dress with little tabs. Then Daddy puts the records on the turntable and everyone dances.

Frankie remembers climbing up to the top bunk with her hand puppet on her right hand. She falls asleep cuddling her new furry toy, feeling grateful that the day has been free from her father's angry outbursts, and hoping that he won't come in the night.

— 5 —

Abandoned and alone

Frankie aged 50 and 2½

Frankie returns to the counsellor one week later ready to talk about that lovely Christmas. But when she starts speaking about Aunty Orla and the games they all played, the counsellor stops her.

"Good memories are great. They put difficult times into perspective, but you only have four more counselling sessions left. Maybe it would be a good idea to spend the time trying to make sense of your distressing memories."

Frankie is quickly transported back to when she was two and a half years old and William had only recently been born. She takes her time, because it really hurts to remember that; her throat, the doctor, and being left for so long. It all hurt.

She is sitting in a train next to her mother. There is an announcement over the loudspeaker as it arrives at a station. Her mummy opens the train door and cautiously feels the edge of the step before descending onto the almost empty platform. Then she gives her hand to Frankie and guides her down the steps. They walk along the platform and up some concrete steps to a busy road. They turn left into a side street, cross over and continue along a pleasant road lined with red-bricked Victorian terraces, all with neatly fenced front gardens. Frankie looks ahead as they walk. The road seems to go on forever. Her mother is very quiet.

After a while, her mother says, "I'm taking you to a really nice hospital where there will be lots of children and toys to play with."

"Will you stay with me?" Frankie tightens her grip on her mummy's hand. Her mother looks a bit strange and unsure, which is not how she usually looks.

"When we get there I'll leave you for just a short while to go and buy you some comics." Her mother's voice sounds a bit strange too, and she is looking at the ground.

Frankie loves comics. She can't read the words yet but she loves to look at the brightly coloured pictures while she listens to the stories. She feels better knowing that Mummy will return to the hospital to read comics to her. They walk in silence until they reach a large open wrought iron gate. They enter and follow a pathway across lush green lawns until they reach three steps up to a giant, brown wooden door with a shiny handle.

Joanna drops Frankie's hand, turns the handle, and pushes the door open to reveal a huge room with a high ceiling and grey walls that meet a speckled floor. At one end, a very smartly dressed lady is standing behind a counter, speaking into a black telephone. Joanna leads Frankie over to the counter and they wait until the smart lady finishes her telephone call, replaces the receiver and turns her attention to them.

"How may I help you?"

Frankie looks around the room while her mother talks to the lady. She sees several shiny wooden benches. It's so quiet that Frankie wonders if this is where dead people live. The thought makes her shudder so she turns back to hear what the smart lady is saying. Then a middle-aged lady in a pale blue dress and a funny white hat comes through a door and walks straight over to Frankie. She crouches down and asks Frankie what her name is.

"Frankie," the child says shyly. She sees her mummy walking away towards the brown door with the shiny handle. Her mummy doesn't look back, and then she is gone. The brown door shuts with a bang.

"Where's Mummy going?" Then Frankie remembers that her mother is going to the shop to buy comics, so she turns to the lady in blue, who takes her hand, picks up the carrier bag that Joanna has left on the floor and guides Frankie through another door into a silent, empty corridor. Their footsteps echo as they walk past black rubber swing doors with round glass windows in the top.

They come to a big room that the lady in blue calls a ward. It smells of disinfectant like Frankie's mummy uses to put in the drains at home. There are silver coloured cot-beds around three of the walls, each neatly made up with a white pillow, a green bedspread and a white sheet that turns over the top of the bedspread. Frankie has never seen such neat beds, with all the bedclothes tucked in tightly, creaseless. Frankie can't resist touching a corner to see if feels like a knife-edge. The lady guides her further into the room. They pass a large wooden table with small chairs around it, and a higher desk at one end where another lady in pale blue is sitting writing.

Outside some large glass doors there is a garden. It is a square, grassed area surrounded by a pathway leading to a patio, and beyond that there is a small pond next to a grass-covered mound covered in trees and bushes. Frankie notices a few colourful flowerbeds that match the bright colours of children's toys scattered across the grass. Several children are playing there.

The lady in blue leads Frankie to a bed next to the glass doors. She tells Frankie that she is a nurse who will look after her. She puts the carrier bag into a little cabinet by the side of the bed. Then they go out into the garden and walk over to a group of children playing with large multi-coloured wooden bricks.

"This is Frankie, Children," the nurse says.

"Hello, Frankie," the children say, but they don't really take any notice of her. The nurse leaves. Frankie begins to wonder when her mummy will return with the comics. After a while they are all called inside, the nurse removes their coats and they sit on the little chairs around the long wooden table. A lady in white gives out plates of food.

"Eat up now, Duck," she says to Frankie.

Frankie eats but keeps glancing over to the black rubber doors. Why is Mummy taking so long to return with those comics?

After dinner a nurse takes Frankie over to her bed, opens the door of the little cupboard and removes the carrier bag. She takes out a toothbrush, toothpaste, face flannel, rectangular box containing a bar of Pears soap, and Frankie's pink slippers. She undresses Frankie, slips a starched white nightdress over her head and puts the slippers on to her feet. They go into a small bathroom at the end of the ward. The nurse lifts Frankie on to a chair. She runs warm water into a washbasin, rubs the soap on to the face flannel, and washes Frankie's face and hands. Then she washes between Frankie's legs, which stings a little and makes Frankie squirm. The nurse peers at her, then dries her and takes her to her bed. Soon a young man in a white coat comes. He has a stethoscope hanging around his neck. The nurse pulls some screens around the bed and Frankie starts to shake. She holds on tightly to the white sheet.

"Will he do what Daddy does to me?" she asks the nurse.

The nurse gently removes her hands from the sheet and pulls back the covers. She lifts Frankie's nightgown up to her waist and gently separates her shaking legs. The young man with the stethoscope leans over and looks. He gives the nurse a small nod then leaves. Frankie sighs with relief as the nurse pulls down her nightgown and tucks her in tightly. When the lights in the ward are turned off Frankie falls fast asleep without thinking of comics or her mother.

Then someone is gently shaking her shoulder.

"Come on, Frankie, it's time to wake up," urges a nurse. This is a strange voice, not her mummy's voice, not Patricia's voice. And this is not her cosy top bunk bed at home. Then she remembers the neat row of tightly made beds. 'I'm in hospital,' she thinks, 'and Mummy is due back with my comics.'

"Come on, Sweetheart, we need to get you ready for the operating theatre," says the nurse encouragingly.

Frankie knows all about theatres. Nan used to go to a theatre in central London. Nan told her all about the people she saw there, especially Norman Wisdom, who used to make her laugh out loud.

Just then, the nurse reappears with a bowl of warm water and washes Frankie. Frankie shivers as the nurse removes the crumpled white nightdress. Butterflies seem to start flying and bouncing around inside her stomach.

"Arms up, Frankie." The nurse slips a strange white gown over Frankie's arms. The gown is open at the back. The nurse puts Frankie's feet into thick green socks, long enough to reach above her shaking knees. She gives Frankie a tiny plastic cup full of pink liquid to drink.

"All ready to go now," the nurse cheerfully proclaims.

Frankie wonders at these strange clothes. Her Nan used to dress up in beaded dresses for the theatre. She'd told Frankie she wore a real fur stole too. Nan had definitely not talked about long green socks.

Two kindly looking men push a trolley through the black rubber doors and come to Frankie's bed. They are wearing green trousers and tops and green upside-down flowerpot shaped hats pulled tightly over their hair. One of the men picks Frankie up, and gently deposits her onto the trolley. "Lay yourself down, Little One. Now let's put this blanket over you to keep you warm on the way to theatre."

Flat on her back and wrapped up as tightly as a newborn baby, Frankie looks around. All the other boys and girls are sitting on the little seats around the wooden table eating bowls of porridge. Her tummy rumbles. She hasn't had breakfast and is really quite hungry, but the trolley is now on the move. The two men in green chat to each other as they move through the long corridors and into the large room with the brown polished wood counter and shiny wooden benches. Frankie's hopes rise but her mummy is nowhere to be seen.

The trolley stops in front of a metal cage. One of the men pushes a button that rings a bell, and Frankie hears a whirring sound. The man slides open the door of the cage and pushes the trolley inside. They are in a kind of cupboard, which Frankie thinks is very odd. The man closes the metal cage and the whirring starts again. Frankie yawns and closes her eyes.

— 6 —

Institutionalised

Frankie aged 2½ and 50

A voice in the distance is calling her name, but she ignores it. She's too tired to respond. She sinks back into the pillow.

"Come on, Frankie, open those eyes," she hears the voice say again. Her throat hurts. She struggles to lift her eyelids but the weight defeats her. Someone is rubbing the back of her hand.

"Try again, Darling," the same voice is closer this time.

With a huge effort she opens her eyes and sees a blurred smiling face.

"Well done, Frankie!" the blurry face says, "Now I'm going to lift your head so you can have a little sip of water."

This is an inviting prospect because Frankie's throat is really sore and her lips are dry. She feels a strong hand slide under her head and gently lift it off the pillow. Something cool touches her lips and cold liquid seeps into her mouth, but then a searing pain hits the back of her throat. She cries out but she has made only a weak croak. She feels the tears form in the corner of her eyes and slide down her face. They collect in a pool in her neck just above the top of her breastbone.

The nurse sitting beside her comes into focus. A wet cloth is passed over her face and neck and that makes things better, calmer. But when she sees blood on the towel she panics and starts crying again.

"Calm down, Sweetie. The nice doctor has removed your tonsils. That's why there is a little blood around your mouth and you are feeling so sore."

Frankie is really awake now and trying to understand. How can the doctor be nice if he made her throat this sore? She is very tired and drifts back to sleep for a bit until she feels the trolley move, the wheels squeaking over the floor below. Again she hears the whirring sound. The cage door opens and she is back in the cupboard. One of the green men smiles at her, but she can't smile back because it hurts too much. When she swallows the searing pain is back and more tears come.

"Don't cry, little girl," the green man says. "You have a treat waiting for you when you get back to the ward. Lovely red jelly and ice cream," he grins. "You do like jelly and ice cream don't you?" Frankie can only nod. The man pats her on the shoulder as they pass through the big room with the shiny wooden benches and carved counter.

Soon she is in her bed in the ward, waiting for the promised bowl of jelly and ice cream. She's given up hope of her mummy returning. When the other children are called to the wooden table for lunch, the nurse pushes a table on wheels to Frankie's bed. The bowl of jelly and ice cream tastes nice and cool but it really hurts to eat it, so she stops after three spoons full. She sighs deeply, leans back on her pillows, and closes her eyes. Footsteps approach. It's the white meals lady.

"I know it hurts to swallow, but the more you do it, the sooner that sore throat will disappear." The lady holds the spoon to her mouth.

Over the next few afternoons lots of mummies and daddies come through the black rubber door, but not Frankie's. Somehow that's all right. She gets used to watching it all between drifting off to sleep in her neat bed.

The first day that she is allowed out to play in the garden, a group of small girls invite Frankie to join a skipping game, and she wins. This makes her feel great, especially when all the girls pat her on the back and say how good she is at skipping. No one has ever told her such nice things before, not even when she did such a good job of handing around the Christmas biscuits.

Two weeks pass. Some of the visitors pop over to Frankie's bed too. One of the mummies gives her some grapes, and another one stays to have a chat. And she is allowed to play in the garden most days. Then, one afternoon the nurse comes out to her and points to two people standing on the patio just outside the glass door of the ward.

"Frankie, guess who's here to take you home?"

Frankie cannot see anyone that she recognises.

"It's your mummy and daddy," explains the nurse. Frankie stays where she is, feeling confused. The nurse leads her by the hand towards the two people who are now waving at her. She barely recognises them. Frederick picks up her carrier bag and all the nurses say goodbye as Joanna takes her hand and leads her out of the ward.

They walk along the road to the railway station in silence. The train journey back home is just as lacking in conversation. Frankie occupies herself by looking out of the window at the passing back gardens.

Frankie's thoughts remain with trolleys, cold jelly and ice cream, and the moment when she did not recognise her parents, until the counsellor says, "What are you feeling right now?"

"Intense sadness."

"Can you put into words why you feel like that?"

"I'm wondering why my parents left me for so long in hospital without once visiting me," Frankie explains, "all the other children's families visited every single day. My parents didn't visit once."

"What do you think might have been their reason?" the counsellor asks.

Frankie desperately wants to find a valid excuse; anything rather than face what she suspects is the truth.

"Maybe it was too far to travel," she suggests, "especially as my father worked such long hours and my mother had my new baby brother, William, to look after."

"Any other reason you can think of?" questions her counsellor.

Suddenly Frankie can't stop the words tumbling out of her mouth.

"My mother lied to me about the comics. She could have stayed with me, but she didn't. It was easier for her to leave. She didn't want to be bothered with a crying child after the operation either."

The counsellor says nothing. She waits for Frankie to go on.

"Also, my parents didn't seem pleased to take me home, did they? I mean they didn't speak to me for the whole journey."

"What are you trying to say?"

"I'm trying to say that they didn't want me back!" Frankie blurts out angrily, feeling tears stinging her eyes. "By then they had the one girl and one boy they always wanted. I was just an unwanted extra mouth to feed!" Frankie tries to calm herself with a couple of deep breaths before she continues,

"… and then there was the incident when the hospital doctor looked at my private parts after the nurse noticed I was sore. Did he realise that something was amiss? Did he just keep his concerns to himself? Why didn't he do something about it? He could have intervened to protect me but he didn't!"

"You're rightly very frustrated about that.'" The counsellor is sympathetic. "But in those days, as you know, nobody spoke of such things and the likelihood was that even if you'd disclosed what was happening, you wouldn't have been believed."

"That's true," agrees Frankie, "but that doctor should have done *something*."

"What happened when you arrived home?" the counsellor asks.

"Patricia came running downstairs and gave me a big hug. It made me feel so loved. Then my grandmother came out of the lounge with William in her arms. She gave me a lovely cuddle. At least two people in this world loved me. Then everything fell back into place and life continued normally as if the hospital bit had never happened."

"We've gone over our hour, Frankie." The counsellor looks up as usual to the wall clock. "The next time we meet, I'd like to better understand what normal life actually meant for you back then."

Frankie says goodbye and leaves in a daze. She remembers very well what normal life was like for her at that time, and the thought of sharing it makes her feel sick.

—7—

What is normal?

Frankie aged 4

Frankie stands in the corner of the kitchen covering her ears with her hands. It is Guy Fawkes Night. She is four years old today. All her relatives are at the house for her birthday party, and as usual it's all about the fireworks. She hates fireworks. The adults are screaming with panic and laughter as they chase each other with bangers and jumping crackers.

Frankie would love to invite friends of her own age to her birthday tea. She imagines little girls arriving in pretty party frocks, each carrying a brightly wrapped birthday present for her. They would sit in a circle on the floor while she opened them. They would play party games like "Poor Jenny is a Weeping", "The Farmer's in his Den", or "Musical Chairs". But Frankie has never had a party like that. Patricia and William have. They were lucky not to be born on Guy Fawkes.

It's fun beforehand, collecting bits of wood and old cardboard boxes to burn on the bonfire, and making the Guy out of old clothes and screwed up pieces of newspaper. This year she made a mask on a stuffed carrier bag, and she pulled an old woolly hat over the top of the Guy's head. But Daddy won't let them take their Guy into the street on a cart

---

like the other kids can do. They could collect money if they were allowed to shout out "Penny for the Guy", but they can't. Daddy says no children of his are begging like that. The bonfire is good, but it's not fun at all when the crackers go off.

After her birthday, everything returns to normal. She wakes from a deep sleep when she senses someone is standing next to her bed. She doesn't need to open her eyes to know who it is. She can hear the heavy breathing. She stays absolutely still. Patricia is asleep in the bed below. Frankie prays that her sister won't wake up and see what is happening. She feels the blankets being loosened. The large warm hand slides between the sheets and moves across her left thigh. The familiar feeling of half dread and half thrill shoots through her like an electric shock. She forces herself to keep breathing as if she were asleep, because he must not know she is awake and dreading. She knows exactly what will happen next. One of her father's hands is on the mound between her legs and his other hand is inside his pyjama trousers. For the next ten minutes she forces herself to stay perfectly still, trying to control the panic and pleasure as she hears her father's breathing get faster and shallower. Then he gives out a small groan and shudders. She knows that he will now withdraw his hand. She hears his soft footsteps heading towards the bedroom door then going down the hall. She feels so dirty and guilty, but surely her father must love her to do that. She takes her confused thoughts back to sleep.

The next morning, at 6 a.m. as usual, her mother shatters the quiet with the vacuum cleaner and the whole household is woken. So another day starts. Daddy goes off to work and returns late, tired and bad-tempered. Little William is always asleep by the time Daddy gets home. Frankie and Patricia know to stay out of the way. Frankie's bedtime is usually right about when Daddy gets home and Patricia has another half an hour because she is the eldest.

That evening Frankie and Patricia are playing together on the lounge carpet. They are already in their warm winceyette pyjamas and thick red dressing gowns. Mummy made those dressing gowns on her Singer treadle sewing machine, so they are not allowed to get the lace-edged collars dirty. Patricia tells Frankie that it's time for her to go to bed, but Frankie doesn't want to yet. Mummy won't notice if she's quiet and they haven't finished their game of snakes and ladders. But Patricia insists, so Frankie makes a face at her and goes to the kitchen to say goodnight to her parents.

As she opens the door, something flies across the kitchen, and Mummy screams. Frankie jumps backwards in horror. Frederick is shouting angrily. Pieces of willow patterned dinner plate lie on the floor. Frankie sees bits of food sliding down the wall next to the door where she is standing. Brown gravy trickles down in a thick smear.

Frankie's father is standing on the doormat at the back door, still fully clad in his thick overcoat, a flat cap on his head, a scarf wrapped twice around his neck and trousers held close around his ankles with bicycle clips. He has come home in a very bad mood and is doing one of his explosions, yelling and yelling. Joanna stands trembling behind the small kitchen counter, eyes wide and hands covering her mouth.

The atmosphere in the room is electric. Frankie is too shocked to move as two pairs of eyes fix on her. She holds her breath in sheer terror. She sees the pure anger in her father's eyes, and senses danger. She tries to move but her legs are frozen. Frederick's eyes are glaring as he moves forwards like a hungry lion stalking its prey. He lifts his right arm, and Frankie instinctively lifts hers to protect her face. Everything feels like it is happening in slow motion. Frankie screws up her eyes and tenses her small body in preparation for the blow, but suddenly Joanna seems to fly across the kitchen, throwing herself between her husband and daughter, and pushing Frankie backwards out of harm's way. Joanna takes the full impact of her husband's blow on her left shoulder.

"Run, Frankie!" implores her injured mother, "Run!"

Frankie turns and runs through the dining room and into the lounge where she sees Patricia's pale, shocked face. She grabs her sister by the arm and drags her up from the floor, "Come on, Patricia!" then continues heading towards the door at the opposite end of the lounge, and straight out into the dark hallway. Patricia overtakes Frankie and pulls her upstairs. Their mother is still screaming and their father is still shouting aggressively. They rush into their bedroom, push the door closed behind them, and leap in a tangle of shivering limbs to hide under the bottom bunk bed. They stay like that for what seems hours before the screaming and shouting from the kitchen dies down and silence prevails.

"Do you think Daddy's killed Mummy?" Frankie whispers into Patricia's ear.

"I don't know."

"Will he come and kill us too?" Frankie asks in a small quivering voice. Patricia tightens her arms around Frankie and puts her finger to her lips. They must keep quiet. It's still quiet downstairs. After another long time Patricia finds the courage to slide out from under the bed. She creeps to the door and peers through the keyhole. She can't see anything. She gets Frankie out from under the bunk and they crawl together into the bottom bunk bed. They are still in their red dressing gowns. Frankie hopes the collar on her gown is not dirty. Mummy would not like that.

Next morning, Frankie and Patricia are woken up by the welcome and comforting sound of the vacuum cleaner. Joanna is still alive. Relief sweeps through them. Stiff from the tension of the night before, they get out of bed and creep hand in hand downstairs. Half way down, they peep over the bannister rail to see if their mother is alone. At that moment the vacuum cleaner stops, and Joanna, seeing two pairs of eyes looking towards the kitchen, beckons to them. They obey and descend the last few steps before gingerly entering the kitchen.

"Hot or cold milk on your cereal, girls?" Joanna says in her normal voice.

"Hot please," they say together. They hesitantly move toward the table. William is already strapped into his wooden high chair, bib around his neck. He is feeding himself with a big messy spoonful of porridge. Patricia looks questioningly towards Frankie, and they both look over to where their mother is warming the milk for their cereal. As she turns around they see her face is swollen and her left arm is hanging limply at her side. Their mother looks embarrassed, as if she had somehow forgotten to wake up with a normal arm. She puts brightness into her voice.

"Sit down you two. We don't want this hot milk getting spilled over you, do we?"

Frankie and Patricia sit and eat their cereal whilst Joanna clears up the mess that William has made. After breakfast the girls return to their bedroom and get dressed. Neither mentions the previous evening, because it's good that Daddy has not killed Mummy, and maybe it won't happen like that again for a while if they are lucky. Best not to talk about it.

Things stay quiet for a couple of weeks. Frankie starts to relax, until one Friday evening. William is in bed as usual when Frederick arrives home from work. Patricia and Frankie are in the lounge. The television is on. After Frederick has had his dinner, he comes into the lounge and sits in his red leather armchair beside the fire. "Pat, go and help your mother in the kitchen," he says.

Frankie starts to feel uneasy when Patricia leaves. She glances at her father and her heart begins to beat harder as she sees a glint in his eyes. Her body tenses as she hears the words she's dreading.

"Come and sit on my lap, Frankie." She obeys without question. She knows that not to obey is likely to send her father into a temper.

Frederick pulls her further on to his lap until she can feel a hardening lump beneath her. She stares unseeingly at the television screen. His warm hand is stroking her nightdress-covered thigh, and then the hand slides under her nightdress. Joanna and Patricia could come back into the lounge at any minute. She keeps her eyes fixed ahead, feeling the hard lump beneath her getting larger and harder. Her father's breathing is getting faster and shallower. She wishes she were somewhere else but is too paralysed to move. What her father is doing to her feels nice, but she also doesn't like it and is embarrassed. He increases the speed of his hand along with his breathing. As soon as Frankie hears him groan, she slips down from his lap and returns to the settee. Moments later Patricia returns.

"Mummy says it's time for you to go to bed, Frankie," she says.

Tonight Frankie doesn't mind that Patricia tells her what to do. She dutifully goes over to kiss her father goodnight and as she leaves the room, she bumps into Joanna who is simultaneously entering. She kisses her mother goodnight, and runs upstairs with relief. As she dives into bed her heart is thumping. She takes several long, deep breaths to slow it down. She wants to sink into a hot bath and scrub and scrub herself clean of the invisible muck that coats her. Her father probably does love her, she thinks, as she starts to feel the floating edge of sleep.

— 8 —

The Revelation

Frankie aged 50

Frankie is embarrassed. She has just finished recounting her description of 'normal' childhood life. She has openly admitted for the first time ever that her father's abusive actions were not an unpleasant experience. She expects the counsellor to look shocked and disgusted. The counsellor doesn't. Instead she asks Frankie how she feels now.

"I feel incredibly guilty but angry at the same time," Frankie replies.

"Can you expand on that a little?"

"Well, I feel guilty for obvious reasons. They call it abuse but everyone thinks of abuse as physical violence, something that causes an injury." Frankie feels the anger welling up inside her. "My injury is invisible to other people. My father played with my head and my emotions. He took away my childhood, my innocence. That bit never heals. It just festers and festers. It amounts to a life sentence. It's almost impossible to rid myself of the twisted idea of what love is and how I should express it. I feel like my father set me up to attract abusers for the rest of my life because I don't know how to respond to men appropriately."

Frankie doesn't realise that her voice has been getting louder and louder. Her emotions are boiling over. She's so angry that she feels a compelling need to hit out at her father and hurt him as much as he hurt her, she can't even do that because he is dead. He escaped the punishment that her very being needs to inflict upon that cruel, perverted and selfish apology for a human being!

She feels the heat rising within her. Her face burns. Perspiration slides down her forehead and into the corners of her eyes, which start to smart. She's trembling and feels as if she is going to burst from the anger inside her. Then the tears come. They wash away the perspiration from her eyes, but now her eyes sting as the mascara drips from her eyelashes.

An arm slides around Frankie's shoulder and holds her tightly. She hears a gentle shushing noise coming from the counsellor who is sitting on the arm of her chair.

"Take some deep breaths, Frankie," she instructs.

Frankie obeys. The anger gradually subsides and is replaced with a feeling of numb shock, quickly followed by intense exhaustion. The counsellor passes her a wodge of tissues. She wipes her eyes, seeing the mascara clotting on the tissues.

"There's a mirror behind you, Frankie," says the counsellor. Frankie stands and turns around, wiping her cheeks until the black 'tramlines' are gone.

"Do you feel able to continue?" the soothing voice enquires.

Frankie realises that although exhausted, she feels somehow lighter. She has set free thoughts that have been haunting her for over forty years, and to her surprise, the world has not spiralled into self-destruction. The counsellor doesn't look in the least bit shocked. She remains as calm as ever. Frankie considers the question for a few seconds and decides that yes, she is fine to continue, and in fact very much wants to.

"Frankie, I want you to know that your feelings, including your anger, are perfectly normal. I also want you to know that you have no need to feel in any way guilty. Guilt is the instrument your father used to keep you quiet when you were a little child. The guilt belongs to *him*, not to you."

Frankie considers this for a few moments and realises that this woman is absolutely right. She nods as the truth sinks in. The counsellor allows her time to absorb the words before she continues.

"You have described what normal life was for you when you were very young, but what part did your mother play in all this?"

"Well, in some ways she protected us kids, like when she got in between my father and me after he'd thrown his plate of dinner across the kitchen that evening." Surely that's true, Frankie thinks, but then she suddenly feels unsure about what she is about to say.

"Go on," says the counsellor gently, "It's okay to voice your thoughts and suspicions if you want to."

"Well, it's just that surely my mother must have wondered what my father was up to when he disappeared out of her bed at night. She wasn't a deep sleeper. She'd be up like a shot if one of us so much as made a sound."

"Was your mother a loving person?" questions the counsellor.

"No, I don't think she was," Frankie says after considering the question. "I have no memory of her ever telling any of us that she loved us. She never hugged us or gave us a spontaneous kiss on the cheek. In fact she was quite a serious person. Come to think of it, I can't remember her ever laughing, although I'm sure she must have at some time."

GLORIA EVELEIGH

"How did you feel towards your mother?" said the counsellor.

"I loved my mother – at least when I was a child I did. In many ways I saw her as the ally of all four of us children. It wasn't until after I got married and moved away from home that my feelings towards her gradually changed. I started to recognise her inability or lack of motivation to protect us from the man that she was supposed to love but seemed frightened of. It wasn't until I had children of my own and I eventually realised I would rather die than let any harm come to them that I began to see her differently. I suspected she had been more concerned about her own safety than that of her three vulnerable children. And yet, even that thought leaves me confused when I think again about how she was willing to risk her own safety to protect me on that plate-throwing evening." Frankie goes quiet. Her thoughts are hurtling towards another idea.

"I believe my mother's behaviour towards me is directly related to the way I felt towards my eldest daughter when she was first born. The instant love that people talk about at the birth of your child didn't happen to me. I had to work at it over several weeks."

The counsellor nodded knowingly.

"And obviously my father's behaviour towards me left me confused about how a normal dad acts towards his kids. Now I watch my present husband interacting with our youngest daughter. It is something innocent and beautiful to observe – a special bond that I never experienced. That fact hurts me almost as deeply as the rest of the abuse. That man stole something so precious from me and I will never get it back."

The counsellor sees Frankie's emotions bubbling to the surface again, and knowing that their hour is coming to an end, she gently brings the session to a conclusion.

"You are right to feel angry, Frankie," she reasons, "only now after so many years are you recognising and voicing those feelings."

She thinks for a few seconds before she continues.

"It might be good to take a closer look at how your mother behaved towards you during your childhood – things like how she communicated both in words and emotions to you and your siblings. You mentioned that as you grew up and moved further away from your parents you started to interpret your mother's actions differently. You also say you blame her for the lack of feelings you experienced at the birth of your eldest daughter."

Frankie can see where this wise woman is leading.

"During the week, Frankie, perhaps you can try to remember an incident that typically demonstrates your mother's behaviour so that we can explore your theory about how this affected you."

For Frankie, who spent the first half of her career as a scientist, this idea holds no fear. It's like a research project with aim, method, results and conclusions. Systems and structures are within her comfort zone.

She says her goodbye and leaves. She feels relaxed and at ease, having given vent to her thoughts and emotions for the first time. That evening she tells her husband about her revelations. He nods sagely.

"I was hoping you'd start to see things for what they really are, Frankie." he says. "Onwards and upwards from here."

"I hope so," she says. But she wonders what else might be buried deep in her subconscious.

— 9 —

A New Era

Frankie aged 5

"Where are we going, Mummy?" There is no response.

"Mummy where are we going?" five-year-old Frankie asks again, as Joanna increases her walking speed, dragging her daughter along beside her.

Again, no response.

Frankie decides not to repeat her question a third time for fear of being lifted off her feet by her mummy walking even faster. Her legs are already moving so fast that she is finding it hard to catch her breath.

Soon she and her mother reach a row of local shops. The first shop is the baker. Frankie manages a split second glance at the marshmallow-filled, chocolate covered cones in the window as she is dragged past. Her mouth waters, because she is sure they are the same chocolate cones she loves when her mummy very occasionally buys them for Sunday afternoon tea.

Next they speed past the butcher's shop with its wood shavings on the floor and whole pigs hanging from hooks on the wall. Then they soon reach the roundabout at the end of the road. Here they turn left to follow another row of shops. They pass the hardware shop that doubles as a post office, the wool shop where Frankie loves to look at the colourful bales of yarn, and then the newsagent that also sells sweets. Finally they stop to join a large group of other mothers and their children.

Nothing seems to be happening except for the sound of general chit-chat. The mothers occasionally peer up the road in the direction of the roundabout.

"Mummy, what are we waiting for?" asks Frankie after a few minutes. Her mother says nothing.

"Mummy..."

"Be quiet Frankie!" interrupts Joanna sternly, "Can't you see I'm talking?"

Just then three coaches circle their way around the roundabout and come to a halt in front of the crowd. Ladies carrying clipboards emerge from the open door of each coach and begin to call out names. Mothers lead their children to the ladies at the coaches, and the coach ladies guide the children up the steps where they disappear inside.

Soon Frankie hears her own name called, and her mummy passes her to a coach lady. Just inside the coach there is a man in a black uniform with a peaked hat. He smiles at Frankie, takes her hand, and leads her to one of the double seats half way down the coach.

"Now you just sit down and shuffle across towards the window," the smiley man instructs. Frankie obeys.

"That's my girl!" he says, and then he returns to the front of the coach.

Frankie looks out of the window to her left. She notices the thinning crowd but she can't see her mummy no matter how hard she looks. She feels confused but also excited because she's never been in a coach before. As the coach moves away some mummies stand on the pavement, craning their necks and waving cheerily, but Frankie's mummy is not there. They left in a hurry this morning, so maybe Mummy has gone back to her vacuum cleaner. Nobody is waving at Frankie. She doesn't know if the other children on her side of the coach are waving back at their mums because the seat backs are too high to see over.

She looks away and turns to the little girl sitting beside her. They study each other carefully and smile shyly. The other little girl has long dark hair, very different to Frankie's own short hair, which is a kind of mousy-blond. Frankie is glad that they both wear similar glasses. They remain silent for the entire thirty-minute journey.

Frankie watches the rows of big, red-bricked houses go by, and then the trees, bushes and grass of the Common. Soon the coach drives over a railway bridge and joins a queue of traffic waiting to turn right into a road bordered on each side by lots of shops. After five minutes Frankie's coach reaches the front of the queue and joins the other traffic heading towards a set of traffic lights. The coach moves into the right-turning lane. While they wait for the traffic lights to turn green Frankie notices a pet shop. The partitioned window is full of small puppies, kittens and rabbits. Frankie wishes she had a pet. If she had a kitten, she would love it and it would love her back, and she would let it sleep on her bed.

Then the coach jolts into action and turns right into another busy road heading towards the town centre. Frankie wonders where they are going. Where is the coach taking her? 'Maybe we are going to the seaside or a big park with swings, roundabouts and see-saws,' she thinks.

Suddenly they come to a halt in front of a two-storey building with lots of identical windows. The building sits in the middle of a flat, tarmacked area surrounded by high, shiny, black metal railings.

"Listen, Children!" It's the voice of the lady with the clipboard. Frankie can't see her but she can hear her words.

"Please stand up and move into the centre aisle to form a neat queue."

Frankie and the other little girl slide out and stand in the aisle. Frankie looks behind and in front of her. All the other children look nervous, and suddenly Frankie is nervous too. She looks again at the building. It looks like Patricia's school.

"Right, Children, please follow me." The clipboard lady disappears down the steps of the coach and the queue of children begins to slowly move forward. Frankie wants to grab the waist of the child in front and shout, "Woo woo!" as if she were playing trains with William.

When the children reach the front of the coach the smiling man in the black uniform and peaked cap helps them down the steps. Once they are on the ground the queue of children snakes its way through the gate and across the tarmac. They reach an archway and enter the building through a large green door.

Inside, the first thing Frankie notices is the smell. It sort of reminds her of pencil sharpener cuttings and her paint box. They reach a large, cold room with rows of small, dark wooden desks and benches. The lady directs Frankie to a desk beside a huge fireplace, with the biggest fireguard she has ever seen. There is a fire in the grate but it doesn't seem to radiate any heat at all. Frankie shivers as she sits down. At the front of the class there is a wooden table and chair, and a large blackboard on the wall. An aquarium sits on a pale blue table-height cupboard to the left of the blackboard. Frankie can see goldfish swimming among the waterweeds. Some fish dart in and out of ceramic arches that are held upright by tiny coloured stones in the bottom of the tank. She is mesmerised by the flashes of gold as the fishes catch the sunlight shining in from the nearby windows.

Now the lady from the coach sits at the table facing the children. She has removed her coat to reveal a straight black skirt and white shirt-blouse. She wears black shoes with small heels. Her spectacles are not on her face but hang around her neck on a black cord. Her brown hair is fastened in a tight bun at the nape of her neck. There is absolute silence in the room as every pair of eyes focuses on her.

"Children, I am your teacher. You will always address me as Miss. This is your classroom. You are in Class 1. You will not speak unless you raise your hand and I give you permission. When you arrive at school each morning, you will come straight to this classroom. You will remove your coats and hang them on one of the hooks at the back. You will remember which hook you have hung your coat on. You will then sit at your desk." The teacher stops talking as she picks up a jug of water and pours its content into a glass beaker. She takes a sip. When she speaks again, she has every child's attention.

"When I point to your row of desks, you will hang up your coat and immediately return to your seat. Do you understand?" Fifty small heads nod. "Do you understand?" the teacher repeats in a sterner voice. Everyone nods again.

"When I ask you a question, you will not nod your head. You will say clearly, 'Yes Miss.' Do you understand?"

This time fifty small voices speak at once. "Yes Miss!"

"That's better." Miss rises from her chair and stands in front of the row of desks nearest to the classroom door.

"Row 1, you go now," she instructs. The children dutifully rise from their benches and do as instructed.

Frankie's row is the last to be told to go and hang up their coats. When Frankie walks to the back of the room and removes her coat, all the pegs have been taken. She panics. There is nowhere for her to hang her coat. Her heart begins to thump inside her chest. She can't breathe properly.

"What is your name, Child?" The teacher has come up behind her.

Frankie begins to tremble. Her mouth is dry. Her words stick in her throat. At last she manages to find a croaky whisper. "Frankie," she says.

"Speak up Child!" demands the teacher.

"Frankie, Miss." Frankie is trembling.

"Give me your coat," the teacher instructs.

Frankie does as she is told and the woman pushes aside a number of coats before she finds a hidden peg. She hangs the coat on the peg.

"Now you make sure you remember where your coat is hanging, Frankie," instructs the teacher as she turns around and returns to the front of the classroom. Frankie follows and gratefully sits back at her desk.

"Now, Children, as it is your first day at school, we will not be joining the rest of the school for assembly in the games hall," the teacher informs the mystified children. "Instead, you will have a treat."

While Frankie wonders what assembly is, Miss is walking up and down the rows of desks, putting something in front of each child. When she reaches Frankie she plonks a lump of grey material on the desk. Frankie does not touch it. Nor do the other children.

Miss sits down at her table and says, "You now have thirty minutes to mould your plasticine into the shape of an animal."

Frankie picks up the grey lump. It feels hard and cold. Many of the other children are trying to warm up their plasticine with their hands. Some are banging it on their desks to soften it. When Frankie bangs hers it stays hard. She tries rolling it back and forth across the surface of her desk to make it into a sausage shape. She does her best to split a smaller piece away from the bigger lump with her fingernails and ends up with a pea-sized piece, which she manages to soften enough to flatten under her thumb. She repeats the process eight times, rolling each piece into a thin sausage shape. She attaches each sausage evenly around the flattened piece to make a spider. It's a funny looking spider but she finishes it just as Miss tells everyone to stop.

"It's now playtime, Children. You may leave your plasticine on your desks. Collect your coats and line up in front of the door."

Everyone scrambles for their coat. Frankie finds her small blue coat lying in a heap on the floor. She slips her arms into the sleeves as she hurries to the front of the classroom to join the other children.

Miss says, "Follow me, Children," and leads the way out of the classroom and along a gloomy corridor to an open door. Outside is an enclosed quadrangular playground. At one end is a toilet block with two entrances, one for girls and one for boys. In a separate area there is a large seesaw in front of a single-storey building. Frankie's eyes open wide with delight and she runs over and climbs onto one end. A young woman approaches.

"You are not allowed in this area, little girl," she says sternly. She lifts Frankie down from the seesaw and gently steers her back towards the school playground. Frankie is embarrassed. She leans against the school wall feeling miserable. She doesn't like this place at all. It's so big and feels so cold and unfriendly.

After a while a loud piercing sound makes Frankie jump. She turns to see a teacher with a shiny whistle at her lips. Most of the children have suddenly stopped running around. They look like small statues as they focus on the teacher who blew the whistle. When the teacher blows for a second time the children start to form themselves into lines. After the third whistle one row of children at a time march back into the school building. Class 1 children are the last to move, and the playground teacher leads them into their classroom where Miss is sitting at her table sipping a cup of tea.

When they have hung up their coats and returned to their desks Frankie realises that she needs to use the toilet. She is too scared to ask Miss, so she sits through the rest of the morning trying to ignore the sensation associated with her dilemma. By the time she has listened to a story and almost finished a drawing she can wait no longer. She raises her hand and stands up, but as she does so, the torrent begins. Her face turns bright crimson and, to her horror, the children around her begin to giggle.

When the teacher sees Frankie standing in a large pool of urine, she rises from her chair and rushes towards her. She says nothing, but gently takes Frankie's hand, leads her to the front of the classroom, opens the door and tells her to wait outside. She goes back into the classroom and, leaving the door open, says to the still giggling children, "Quieten down. I want you to sit and carry on with your pictures until I return."

In the corridor Frankie is quietly sobbing. The teacher takes her hand and leads her to a small room where a nurse is sitting at a table. The nurse immediately jumps to her feet and comes over. The teacher has a few quiet words with her before she disappears back to Class 1.

"Hello Frankie," says the nurse. She guides Frankie towards a washbasin. "Let's clean you up, shall we?" She replaces Frankie's knickers with a pair of boys pants, rinses the wet knickers under the warm tap, squeezes them out, and wraps them up in newspaper. Frankie thinks of the fish and chips at the seaside. She hopes she won't have to give the newspaper parcel to her mummy.

To Frankie's surprise, the nurse does not return her to the classroom but instead takes her to a cosy room next door.

"Frankie, this is Mrs Green. Mrs Green is the headmistress. You will stay with her until home time." The headmistress comes out from behind her desk and leads Frankie to an armchair in front of a large fireplace where tall flames are playing. This fireplace is warm.

"Here you are, my love," she says to Frankie, "Warm up in front of the fire." A large long-furred cat wanders over and jumps up onto Frankie's lap. This is heaven, Frankie thinks. She strokes the soft, purring creature and as the heat from the fire slowly warms her face, she leans back and falls into a peaceful sleep.

She wakes with a start. "Good gracious, you're still here!" exclaims the headmistress, "I'd forgotten all about you. I hope your coach hasn't already left." There is a knock at the door.

"Come in," says the headmistress.

It's Frankie's teacher holding her small pupil's blue coat.

"Come on young lady," her teacher says. She helps Frankie into her coat, picks up the newspaper package that is sitting on a coffee table in front of Frankie's armchair, and leads her to the coach that is already full of chattering children. Every small face turns towards Frankie as she climbs up the steps of the coach and sits in the front row next to Miss. She keeps her eyes down all the way home, but she can't help glancing at the newspaper package on her teacher's lap. It is a packet of embarrassment and shame. What will her mummy say?

When the coach arrives back at the drop-off point, all the children get off before Miss rises from her seat. She takes Frankie down the coach steps and over to where Joanna and Patricia are standing beside William in his pram. Miss explains about Frankie's unfortunate accident. To Frankie's horror Joanna laughs and shows the package to all the other mums. They laugh too. Frankie wants to sink into the ground with embarrassment, but instead she keeps her eyes down until they move off. She then takes a surreptitious look at Patricia who smiles at her sympathetically.

That evening, Joanna describes in detail to Frederick all about the accident. He starts to laugh too, especially when Frankie's cheeks turn slowly pink. Patricia, who is sitting next to her on the floor, slides her hand over Frankie's without even looking round at her. Frankie wonders if her parents have any warmth or understanding in them. She goes to bed feeling sad and is glad when the family seems to have forgotten all about the incident by the next morning. She relaxes. But when she gets to the school coach her mother hands a package containing the boy's pants over to her teacher, explaining loudly that she has washed the pants in case another child needs them. Everyone on and off the coach hears, so Frankie spends another journey staring into her lap and wondering how she will survive. Even the nice man in the peaked cap heard what her mother said.

— 10 —

Bully on bully

Frankie aged 50

"So there you are," states Frankie flatly as she concludes her memory of her first day at school, "That was my mother – unable to communicate appropriately on any level really."

"How did you feel about that at the time, Frankie?" asks the counsellor.

"I just accepted it," Frankie answers, "I loved my mum when I was a child. I accepted whatever life threw at me and just thought it was normal."

"How do you feel about your mother's behaviour now?"

"In practical terms she was a good mother although very inflexible in that she had a strict routine and nothing could change that. Hence our rude awakening by the sound of her vacuum cleaner at six o'clock every morning except Sunday," Frankie explains, "I don't think she was able to empathise with us children so was little support in an emotional crisis."

"Did she ever abuse you or your siblings?" the counsellor asks.

"Not unless you count giving us regular good hidings when we stepped out of line. One slap on the bottom wasn't good enough for her. It was one hard slap on the top of our legs for every word she said," Frankie remembers, "but times were different then. Smacking was the accepted form of punishment. Us kids just hoped that her sentences wouldn't be too long!"

Frankie and the counsellor laugh.

"Did you eventually manage to settle down at school, Frankie?"

"No, not at that first school. I was unhappy there for the whole year. It was such a relief when I was able to start attending a local school at the age of six. I settled immediately and would have been very happy except for two things."

"Go on," the counsellor urges.

"Well, the first thing was that I had to walk home for lunch and back again every day because my mother didn't want to pay for school dinners. That would have been okay except for the dogs. I was terrified of dogs. There always seemed to be at least one dog on that walk. I was so scared that I couldn't stop myself from taking flight, and of course as soon as I ran away, the dogs would think I was playing and run after me. It was a nightmare. I would arrive home or back at school out of breath and covered in perspiration."

"That must have been an alarming experience for you."

"Yes it was, but I kept my fear to myself because I was more scared of the other children making fun of me. You'll be pleased to hear that I've grown out of that fear now," Frankie says jokingly.

"Was there an incident that triggered that fear of dogs?"

"Apparently a dog jumped up onto my pram when I was a baby," Frankie answers, "but I have no memory of that so I don't really see how that could have caused it."

"And what was the second thing?" the counsellor asks.

"Miss Finer," Frankie declares sternly, "she was my teacher and she was a real bully."

"In what way?"

"She would take the class into the games hall each day for physical education, and divide us into four groups. One group would do climbing, balancing beam and ropes, while the others would do skipping, quoits, or gymnastics on the mats. We had to change every ten minutes so that we all got a go on everything."

"Sounds like a fairly normal practice."

"Yes it was, but I was a skinny child with little strength or energy. We were often a bit hungry when we were kids. There was no spare food for snacks, and sometimes we didn't get to finish all our dinner because my father would have an explosion and we would have to run and hide. I was a bit of a weakling physically. I was never very good at physical activities of any sort. The worst activity of all for me was the mats."

"What was bad about the mats?"

"Miss Finer wanted every child in the class to be able to do a forward roll. I called it head-over-heels. It made me dizzy every time I tried it, so I was really scared of it. Every other child in the class did their forward roll without a problem. Miss Finer was really annoyed that I couldn't do it. She would take me to the front of the games hall and call everyone's attention to the fact that I could not do a forward roll."

"That was pretty mean."

"And she didn't stop there. She would make me try over and over again while all the other children watched and giggled. Every time I tried, I chickened out at the last moment."

"That sounds like torture. How did you deal with it?"

"I worried and worried for a very long time. Often I couldn't eat or sleep just thinking about the physical education lesson. Every day was horrible because of that."

"Did you say anything to your parents?"

"Eventually my parents noticed I was broody and unhappy and asked me what was wrong. The whole thing came tumbling out one night after dinner. I told them how awful she was to me."

"Did they do anything about it?"

"My father cycled to the school one morning, with me sitting on the cross bar of his pushbike. He went straight in and spoke to Miss Finer, who acted very surprised about the whole thing, as if I had been making it up and it was all in my mind only. However, she never bullied me again. I was so relieved about that."

"So your father rescued you on that occasion," Frankie's counsellor suggests.

"Yes, looking back it seems quite paradoxical, doesn't it? One bully complaining about another!"

Frankie then begins to giggle. "The funny thing is that just a couple of weeks later, my sister and brother managed to teach me to do that dreaded forward role. I think it was easier for me to learn once the pressure was off."

"So apart from those two issues, how was school life in general for you?" asks the counsellor.

"After that I thoroughly enjoyed school. I was quite an intelligent child and found all the lessons very easy. I loved chanting the times tables with the other children in our arithmetic classes. I was good at nature and science, and good at writing stories. Also I really enjoyed acting. My only real difficulty was my poor spelling. We had a spelling test every Friday morning and that hung heavily over me all through the week leading up to it."

"What was home life like around that time, Frankie?" asks the counsellor.

"More of the same really. The sexual abuse continued quite regularly, and we would all walk on eggshells most of the time so as not to upset my father and trigger his violent behaviour. It was not uncommon for him to attack my little brother, especially at meal times. William would be sitting there quietly eating when something he did or said started my father on one of his rampages. He would lean over the table, knocking the food everywhere, and start to thrash my brother. Once he started, my mother would usually scream at the three of us to run up to the bathroom and lock ourselves in. Sometimes my father would chase us up the stairs with my mother trying to hold him back, but we always managed to lock the door just in time. Those times were terrifying for us, and very confusing too, especially for William. Rarely did we know what made our father so angry."

The counsellor leans back in her seat and summarises.

"Okay, Frankie. So life was mostly good at school, if not always at home. All through your childhood you were experiencing sexual and physical abuse, and witnessing your father's violence towards others in your family. "

"Yes," says Frankie. "This upset all of us siblings but it happened so often that it just became part of normal life for us."

The counsellor nods and looks thoughtful.

"Our time is up for today. We have only one more session left, so next week it would be good to focus on any other times that really upset you, so we know it all. I want you to have the opportunity to vent any more emotions that might still remain inside you."

Frankie nods, feeling uneasy about setting herself up to experience more extreme emotions, but she smiles and says goodbye. She walks away from the counselling room with a sense of foreboding. The coming week is likely to be a very unsettling one for her.

She walks back to the office, trying to think about areas of her life not yet revealed to the counsellor. Then she realises that she hasn't mentioned the two people that meant most to her in her childhood, her maternal grandmother and grandfather. Even now, at the age of fifty, she often thinks about Nan and Granddad with great affection. She doesn't yet know that these two dear people will feature in her first dream of the week.

—11—

The dawning of truth

Frankie aged 8

Every other Saturday, Frankie happily sets out on the long walk to Nan and Granddad's house. She carries her nightdress and dressing gown in a brown paper carrier bag and clutches her three-penny piece pocket money in her hand. On the way she visits the sweet shop, with its eight-paned windows. The ping sounds as she opens the door, so that old Mr Williams knows she's there. Frankie studies the shelves packed with large jars twinkling in the light from the window. She knows immediately what she will purchase today because they are Nan's favourites.

"Two ounces of pear drops, please," she tells the shopkeeper excitedly.

Frankie breathes in the distinct lemon smell as the shopkeeper pours out the sunshine-yellow, sugar-coated sweets into the shiny metal dish of the weighing scales. He transfers them into a small white paper bag. He seals it at the top with a tight twist, and swaps it for Frankie's threepence.

"Here you are, my love," he says with a broad, whiskery grin, "and you mind how you go."

It's hard to stop herself from popping one of the pear drops into her mouth while she walks, but she resists because she will enjoy them more if she shares them with Nan. As she gets closer, she can see Nan standing on the step outside her front door watching out for her. Frankie's spirits soar. She runs towards Nan and gets a welcoming hug, something she never gets at home. It's even better when they get inside. Frankie feels her Nan and Granddad's house settle around her like a warm and cosy cloud that never sheds rain. Granddad always gets home late because of work, so Frankie and Nan have lots of time together, and it's lovely. Nan makes her feel special.

One of the things Frankie enjoys most is sitting next to Nan on a chair under the veranda outside the kitchen door. Together they top and tail the gooseberries, redcurrants or blackcurrants, and pod the peas or slice the runner beans from the garden. Nan and Frankie chat away happily as they drop the prepared fruit and vegetables into separate colanders on the floor between them. Sometimes they suck on pear drops and chat at the same time. They have a connection as natural and strong as steel to a magnet. It's never like this with her mother and that makes Frankie sad, but it's always lovely with Nan.

While the meat roasts in the gas oven, Nan shows Frankie how to cook and mash potatoes. Nan is very cuddly, but she is strong enough to really mash those potatoes.

"Now for the gravy, the most important part of the meal," Nan says.

Together they mix the juices from the meat with gravy powder and a crumbled stock cube until the thick brown liquid begins to bubble. Frankie looks up at her Nan's face. Her cheeks are pink from the heat of the stove, her silver hair is hanging in wisps by her ears, and she grins at Frankie as she dishes up the meal. Then she dips a teaspoon into the bubbling gravy, blows it gently to cool it down, and offers it to Frankie to taste.

"Enough seasoning?" Nan asks Frankie with a mock serious look on her face.

"Just a sprinkle more pepper I think," says Frankie, giggling because in this game you are supposed to look serious but she can't.

Nan and Frankie eat in the dinning room, chatting as they enjoy the results of their cooking. Granddad never gets in from work until seven o'clock. His meal remains in the kitchen, sitting on top of a large saucepan of simmering water and covered by a saucepan lid that Frankie lovingly put in place. Frankie would never want to do that for her father. She hasn't earned her father's love even though she has tried so hard. So she wouldn't put a lid on his meal to keep it warm.

Mickey the black cat, who has been snoozing on one of the two dark green easy chairs either side of the hearth, stretches, jumps down from his make-do bed and leaps onto the seat next to Frankie. Stretching over to stroke Mickey's soft fur, Frankie tells him, "Be patient, Mickey. Nanny will give you your dinner when we have finished. Look I'm saving you some meat and gravy, so be a good boy while we eat our food."

After dinner, and once Mickey has been fed with the leftover scraps, Frankie changes into her nightdress and dressing gown, and Nan gets the Snakes and Ladders game from the sideboard cupboard.

"The washing up can wait till later. Let's enjoy ourselves until Granddad gets in."

For the next hour they enjoy rattling the dice in its little cup, cheering when either of them throws a six, and laughing as each overtakes the other in their quest to win. They are still laughing when they hear the sound of a key turning in the front door lock.

"Granddad's home!" shouts Frankie as she jumps down from her chair and runs out into the hallway to greet him. A slim man with a receding hairline, Granddad has high cheekbones just like Mummy's. He smiles broadly at his granddaughter as he removes his coat and hat. Frankie takes him by the hand and escorts him into the dining room where Nan has cleared the table. As Granddad sits down, Frankie moves her chair right next to his before she climbs onto it. Nan brings in Granddad's dinner, complete with a small jug full of the reheated gravy she and Frankie made earlier. She smiles at her husband as she pours it over his food and receives a knowing wink in return.

Frankie chatters away happily, telling Granddad everything that happened today. He smiles and eats his meal. Every now and again he forks up a small morsel of food from his plate and offers it to Frankie, who continues to chew and chat simultaneously. Frankie has learnt that she won't be chastised for this as she would be at home, where Mummy is always saying not to talk with your mouth full.

Nan and Granddad listen with interest to everything she has to say. Occasionally, Granddad pours some tea from his cup into his saucer, blows it cool and lets Frankie drink from it. Bedtime always arrives too soon but Frankie allows Nan to take her up to the spare bedroom and tuck her into the soft single bed, pulling the thick eiderdown over her for extra warmth. Nan sits on the edge of the bed and holding Frankie's hand asks, "What story shall we have tonight, Darling?"

"Tell me a story about you when you were a little girl, Nan."

So the story begins. Frankie can see that Nan gets as lost in it as she does. She loves how Nan continues to affectionately stroke her hand. By the end of the story Frankie is almost asleep. Nan leans over and gently kisses her before quietly leaving the room. Frankie knows that Nan tries to make up for how things are at home.

Sometimes Frankie and Patricia spend the weekend at Nan and Granddad's together. On those weekends Nan and Granddad take the girls to the Workingman's club at the end of the next road to watch the Saturday night dancing. Nan helps them dress up in pretty white crocheted dresses and ankle socks that she made herself. Nan wears a little black dress and gold jewellery, and Granddad dresses in his smart suit with white shirt and striped tie.

At the club they meet friends and sit around a couple of small square tables covered in half-full glasses of beer and spirits. Granddad orders lemonade for Patricia, orange squash for Frankie and buys two packets of crisps. They shake salt from little blue sachets onto the crisps. This is a happy, noisy, laughing place, where Nan loves to be at the centre of the fun while Granddad sits quietly sipping his beer, now and again giving Nan a loving wink. The girls love to see that. Frankie hopes that Patricia is happier at home than she is. She does not know that Patricia is wishing the same for her.

At the club a man with a microphone stands on the stage and introduces the band for the evening. Nan and Granddad sit with Frankie and Patricia while other people get up to dance. Then it's their special moment. The man with the microphone asks if anyone wants to sing. Nan proudly stands up and escorts Frankie and Patricia to the front of the hall and up the three wooden steps on to the stage. The man introduces the sisters and a hush descends over the audience. All eyes turn towards the little girls as they begin to sing into the microphone.

When their song comes to an end, the audience erupts into cheers. Frankie and Patricia smile broadly as they curtsy and prepare to leave the stage, but they have to do an encore. Nan is so proud of them. She hugs them and buys them another soft drink and more crisps. Frankie feels warm and emotional as she looks around the hall. 'All these people who don't even know me make me feel more special than my own mum and dad ever do,' she thinks. All she did was sing and they love her. Frankie shivers as she puts away the thought that something is badly wrong at home.

When they later walk back to Nan and Granddad's house, Frankie knows that she couldn't feel happier than she does right now. Nan and Granddad are the two people she loves most in the world.

— 12 —

Lonely and heartbroken

Frankie aged 9

"No!" screams a voice in Frankie's head, "No, no, no! It can't be true!" The colour drains from Frankie's face. Beads of perspiration form on her upper lip. She pinches her arm hard. She feels the pain. So she's not dreaming. But what she just heard is impossible. She's sitting in an armchair in the lounge reading and she has just heard Nan telling Mum she is moving up north.

"I'm sorry Joanna but your sister, Georgina, needs me right now and I must go to her," says Nan. "I have put the house up for sale so me and your father can raise our half of the deposit for the newsagent shop they want to buy. I will be their business partner."

Frankie looks up and sees that Nan is serious. She has that strong, calm look of having made up her mind about something.

"Firstly, Georgina is not my real sister," states Joanna in a slightly raised voice, "She is my adopted sister."

Nan looks hurt.

"Secondly, you are missing the point!" Joanna says. "Georgina is, as usual, after your money. If you do this, you will end up with nothing."

"We'll have our own rooms in the flat over the newsagent and I'll have a job helping out in the shop," explains Nan in a tone that Frankie has never heard her use before, "Or are you and Frederick just worried that if we do this, then it's you that will have nothing?"

"How can you say such a thing?" replies Joanna trying to keep control of her obvious anger.

Frankie sees a teardrop land on the book she is pretending to read. She looks down as the first teardrop is joined by another and then another. Lifting her hand to her cheek, she discovers the tears are hers. She hastily attempts to wipe them away with the back of her hand but it's too late. Nan looks round and immediately realises that Frankie is silently crying.

"Now look what we've done," she says to Joanna, "we've upset Frankie."

"Frankie shouldn't be eavesdropping, so it's her own fault," proclaims Joanna. She leaves the room, slamming the door behind her.

Nan walks over to Frankie and scoops her up in her arms. She sits on the sofa with her granddaughter on her lap and holds her close as she rocks her from side to side. Nan is sobbing too. After five minutes, Nan looks into Frankie's wet eyes. Slowly and deliberately, she says, "Frankie, you know how much me and Granddad love you, don't you?"

Frankie nods.

"We have to move to a place that is a long way from here because Aunty Georgina needs us even more than you right now," Nan explains, "but that doesn't mean we will stop loving you."

Frankie listens to Nan's words with incredulity. 'How can Nanny love me and leave me?' she thinks. 'How will I cope without our special weekends to look forward to?' The thought of life without Nan is too much. This time the tears come from a place deep within her, accompanied by heaving sobs. Just then Joanna returns from the kitchen to find her mother cuddling her sobbing daughter.

"Run upstairs to the bathroom and wash your face, Frankie," she orders in a stern voice, "you're becoming more of a cry baby everyday."

Frankie flies upstairs at double speed, and rushes into her bedroom where she climbs the wooden ladder and throws herself onto her top bunk bed. She buries her face in her pillow and continues to sob. She hears more talking downstairs, and then Nan is saying, in a loud, flat voice, "You've no need to worry, Joanna. You won't go short." Then there is the sound of Nan leaving and the door not quite slamming.

When Frankie stops crying, she climbs down, stands in front of the window and stares out. She sees nothing but a picture of her own sad and lonely life from now on. She keeps repeating in her mind, 'Nan and Granddad are leaving me, Nan and Granddad are leaving me...' but she cannot make herself believe that it is really going to happen. She now knows that home is not normal. But every plan she has made to improve life has included Nan and Granddad. How can she change things now if Nan and Granddad leave her? Frankie is condemned to live here until she is old enough to get a job and leave home, and it's too much to bear. She is lonelier than ever before. Her heart hurts, really hurts.

Several weeks pass and Frankie and Patricia do not spend a single weekend at Nan and Granddad's because it must be kept tidy for viewings. Then it is sold. Frankie dreads the day when Nan must finally leave. And that day comes. She stands on the pavement with the rest of the family outside the house that was her refuge for so long. Nan, with tears in her eyes, hugs and kisses each child in turn and tells them to go and kiss Granddad goodbye. A final hug for Joanna sees both women openly crying. After a couple of minutes, Nan pulls away from her daughter, touches Frederick's arm and gets into the back seat of the taxi next to Granddad. As the car pulls away, all that Frankie can see is Nan's arm waving out of the open window. Frankie waves back half-heartedly until the vehicle turns the corner at the end of the road, taking her main source of love and happiness away. Everyone remains on the pavement until Frederick says, "Come on now. We can't stand here all day."

Like obedient soldiers they all turn around and follow him home. Frankie has never experienced grief like this before. She fixes her eyes on the paving stones and wonders if she would rather be dead. Then a hand takes hers and holds it firmly. Patricia is walking by her side. They each manage a wan smile. Squeezing each other's hands gives strength. They have each other.

They lift their heads. They will walk forward together.

— 13 —

A brief taste of happiness

Frankie aged 9½

"Run!" shouts Patricia as she grab's William from the clutches of their father and makes for the door to the hallway. Frankie simultaneously jumps up from the sofa where she has been cowering since the commotion started.

All three children thump up the stairs. Frederick is close behind, and Joanna close behind him, trying to grab a handful of his sweater to slow him down. It looks funny, but it is far from funny. This time the rage flared up so quickly that Joanna was unable to get into the lounge in time to protect William. Patricia, at almost thirteen years old, was brave enough to grab William.

All three children manage to get into the bathroom and close and lock the door a split second before Frederick crashes into it. They hear their mother trying to calm their raging father, but he continues to thump on the door and scream at his children for what seems like hours. Why don't their neighbours ever come and knock on the door to see if everything is all right? Frankie thinks maybe the neighbours are scared of Frederick too. Outside the bathroom door Joanna is eventually successful as always, but not without injury. This time he smashed her nose. Yet all this is almost normal to Patricia, Frankie and William.

Without Nan and Granddad around, there is no escape from these regular horrors. Frankie now relies solely on school for her respite. She throws all her energy into doing well. Her end-of-term school reports are glowing but this doesn't change anything at home. Not even good reports could earn her parents' love. The incidents continue, frightening and scarring.

Sexual abuse continues too, gradually becoming more intrusive and persistent. Frankie's tangle of confusion tightens. Her only defence is to disappear to a place deep in her mind whenever things get too much for her. Her self-esteem is at a really low ebb. She spends more and more time with her precious walky-talky doll, brushing its shiny blond hair, dressing it each morning and undressing it and putting it in its wooden cot at night, even though she is a big girl of more than nine now. Her dolls become her family.

Sometimes, while the children are getting ready for school, the postman rings the doorbell. They run downstairs. Whoever reaches the door first has the excitement of receiving the padded brown envelope that heralds gifts from Nan. Joanna opens the envelope and dips her hand inside. She withdraws the folded sheets of notepaper and starts to read. The children fidget with excitement as the suspense intensifies. Each is hoping that the letter is not too long. Their mother then takes a second dip into the depth of the padded envelope and withdraws three small gifts. It is usually a bag of sweets for each of them. Frankie loves these moments. It's as if the package contains a little bit of Nan and Granddad come to visit. Sometimes she receives an item of clothing for her doll, and she takes her gift up to her bedroom and chats away to the doll as she dresses it. Over the months she builds up a complete set of pale blue crocheted clothes. But when she thinks of the Nan who sent the clothes, her heart aches.

Very occasionally they take the car and all visit Nan and Granddad in Bedford. Frederick is an angry and impatient driver. Frankie always gets carsick and that makes Frederick even madder. He refuses to stop when Frankie gets nauseous, and he becomes more and more angry with every other motorist on the road, so Frankie invariably vomits over herself. Her mother has to lean over from the front seat to clean her up as best she can, but the smell stays and makes the rest of the journey unpleasant for everyone.

Once they get to Bedford, things improve. Nan rushes out to meet them and gives each child a warm enveloping cuddle as they emerge one by one from the car. The smell of Nan's perfume draws Frankie back to the hugs she used to enjoy when she spent those precious weekends with her. Auntie Georgina, Uncle Sam, and their children, Laura and Gerald, are waiting in the lounge and jump up from their seats in welcome. The hugging starts all over again.

The house behind the shop is so large, with its three floors and numerous stairs to climb, that the five children can lose themselves within its various rooms. They imagine they are Enid Blyton's Famous Five, re-enacting many make-believe adventures.

Frankie loves the shop, even though it has taken Nan away from her. To her it is a magical place. She has always enjoyed playing shops with the neighbour's two children at home, but here in Bedford the shop is real. Frankie is allowed to serve customers. She hands over their purchases of chocolate or sweets, although they go to Nan to pay.

She feels very grown up when a customer enters and she puts Nan's teaching into practise.

"Good morning. How may I help you?" she asks in her clearest, most grown up voice.

"Good morning, Young lady," reply the customers, happy to go along with her. "Thank you for such a lovely welcome into your amazing emporium. May I have a sixpenny bar of chocolate, please?" Frankie isn't too sure what an emporium is, but not wishing to display her ignorance, she goes over to the display of chocolate on the counter and asks, "Is there a particular make of chocolate you'd prefer?"

"This one will do fine thank you," replies the customer, pointing at the chosen brand.

Frankie, the young shopkeeper, picks up the chocolate bar and places it inside a white paper bag as Nan has shown her. She hands it over to the customer. "That will be sixpence please. Would you kindly pay the cashier."

"I will indeed, young woman, and thank you very much for your expert help," comes the response.

When Nan takes the money she opens the drawer of the till with a ping, and thanks the customer. "Do come again," she says. The customer always gives Frankie a wink or a smile on the way out. It is all so exciting and fun! And Nan always says something like, "Frankie, you are amazing! If you lived up here all the time, I would definitely employ you as my shop assistant!"

That sort of praise makes Frankie very happy. She thinks back over the happy times she spent at Nan's other house. She recalls the piano in the front room – the 'best room' as Nan called it. She sees Nan lifting the lid of the shiny wooden instrument and sitting on the padded piano stool before turning to Frankie to ask, "What will it be tonight, Young Lady?" Frankie always asked for 'She'll be coming round the mountain when she comes'. Nan would raise her hands above the keyboard in the way of a concert pianist, and play a chord, which was Frankie's signal to start singing. They would sing at the top of their voices, and at the end, they would applaud themselves, and begin again with another song. Later, from her bed in the spare room upstairs, Frankie would hear Nan playing beautiful melodies on her much-loved piano. Now she had to go to Bedford and be sick in the car before she saw Nan, but she loved the shop.

"Are you coming to the dancing lesson, Frankie?" Her cousin, Laura, brings her back to the present. There is a ballroom next to the shop.

Frankie is shy and cautious about trying new things, and is not sure about the dancing, but she doesn't want to be left out, so she agrees. Patricia and Laura lead the way through the shop and into the ballroom foyer. Patricia pays at the ticket booth and they all go through the double-doors into the large dance space. At the front they stand among a crowd of other children and stare at the most beautiful people Frankie has ever seen.

The lady is tall and slim, and wears a stunning pink dress with a multi-layered skirt of pink net and silk that matches the pink silk fitted bodice. Her dress ripples with style. Her shoes have really high heels, and glitter with tiny glass crystals that reflect the light from the chandeliers. Her blonde hair is perfect too, brushed back and kept firmly in place with a pink slide covered in the same crystals. The gentleman next to her is also slim and tall. His shoes don't glitter, they shine. He wears a smart black suit and a bright pink bowtie. The lady gently talks into a microphone on a headset. "Welcome, Children."

"Now, Children," directs the shiny-shoed gentleman, "please move to the side of the hall as we demonstrate today's dance, the waltz."

Frankie is spellbound as the graceful pair moves smoothly around the hall. She watches every swoop and step and slide until the music stops. The lady and the man are so beautiful!

Then Frankie looks around and sees that many of the girls are wearing smaller versions of the teacher's dance dress, and several boys are wearing shiny, black shoes just like the gentleman. She is suddenly nervous. She looks down at her well-worn floral cotton dress, passed down from her sister. She feels embarrassed and conspicuous and suddenly wants to leave. When Patricia, dragging William behind her, joins the other children in front of the teachers, Frankie sits down on one of the red velvet padded chairs placed around the edge of the room. She is relieved when nobody notices. She enjoys watching the others. She grins when some children get their legs in a tangle and trip over their own feet. It is probably hard to watch the beautiful people and do the steps at the same time. When the lesson finishes an hour later Frankie joins her family group as they follow the crowd out of the ballroom. Nobody says anything about her absence from the waltz lesson.

One morning Uncle Sam invites Frederick and the children to join him for a day's fishing. Frankie thinks fishing is much less scary than dancing and wants to go with her father. Frederick decides after they've been there for a while that he hates fishing, and doesn't hold back in letting his brother-in-law know.

"What a boring pastime!" he exclaims to the horror of his listening daughter. But fortunately Uncle Sam ignores Frederick's rudeness. Frankie sits on the grass staring at the reflections on the mirror-like surface of the river, wishing it were this calm at home, and trying to ignore her father's regular complaints. That worked for a bit until Uncle Sam got fed up and they went home.

The day of departure brings heartbreak for Frankie all over again. The tight hug and kiss from Nan, and the ruffle of her hair and wink from Granddad prompt her tears. From the back seat of the car she watches Nan and Granddad getting smaller and smaller in the distance as her father drives away. She dare not let Frederick see her crying, as he would scold her for being such a baby.

So they drive away from fishing, and watching beautiful dancers, and working in the shop, and being loved, towards home, where plates are thrown and there are visits in the night, and the vacuum cleaner starts up at six o'clock in the morning.

After that trip to Bedford, Frankie sometimes walks down to her Nan and Granddad's old house just to make her feel closer to them. This helps a little until her mother tells her that the man who now owns the house recently hung himself in the garage. After that Frankie is too scared to ever walk past Nan's house again.

— 14 —

A new life

Frankie age 10

"I'm going to have a baby."

Joanna looks at Frankie and the others to gauge their reaction. They look back at their mother with blank expressions on their faces.

"Do you understand what I'm saying, Children?" Her voice is flat and depressed.

Frankie understands the words, but her mother doesn't look very happy. Surely having a baby is an exciting thing.

"In just a few months, you will all have a new baby brother or sister."

When Frankie hears that she feels wonderful. Her heart suddenly soars at the thought of a real live, responsive baby for her to cuddle, in place of her unresponsive dolls. At the same moment, the good news dawns on Patricia and suddenly the room erupts as both girls simultaneously jump to their feet squealing with pleasure. They almost strangle Joanna with their excited hugs. They cannot think of anything more welcome and shocking. Patricia and Frankie try to pull William into their strange entangled jumping hug, but he looks a bit confused. He's the youngest, and he won't be the youngest anymore.

"Who wants a screaming baby in the house, anyway? Wet nappies, smells, noisy nights!" he says.

After that great news, time goes slowly for Frankie. She is impatient to see her new little brother or sister. She is glad when grey skies and piles of leaves on the ground replace cheery sunshine because she knows that means the time is getting closer. The thought of the new baby sweeps away the blues she has because of missing Nan and Granddad so much. She values every opportunity to touch her mother's expanding bulge. She often feels the kicks and movements of her unborn brother or sister.

Eventually the long awaited day arrives. Frederick tells his children over breakfast that the baby will be born today. Frankie's knowledge of childbirth is very sketchy and she is bemused to find her mother still laying in bed when she goes upstairs to kiss her goodbye before leaving for school. Joanna says that the new baby is likely to have arrived by the time they get home.

Frankie can't concentrate at school and at 3.15p.m. when her class is released she rushes home as quickly as she can. Arriving quite out of breath, she runs straight upstairs and into her parent's bedroom. There, laying in a hand-made wooden and fabric cradle on the far side of her parent's bed is a tiny baby. Her tired mother beckons Frankie to approach the cradle.

"Come and meet your new baby sister, Janet."

Frankie's heart misses a beat as she looks down at the tiny little baby girl and instantly falls in love with her. Looking back up at her from the cradle are two large brown eyes. Frankie touches a tiny hand and smiles as the little fingers wrap themselves around her index finger and grasp it tightly. Just then, her sister and brother enter the bedroom and join her at the cradle.

"It's got a wrinkly, red face," observes William. He screws up his nose with disgust and leaves to do something more interesting. Frankie moves aside to make space for Patricia, whose eyes fill with tears as she sees Janet for the first time. She too experiences the finger-grasping treatment and shares a giggle with her younger, but no longer youngest sister.

"She has lots of black hair," Patricia observes, stroking the soft, silky spikes as she speaks.

Both girls are entranced by their tiny sister and cannot take their eyes off her. Then Joanna tells them she needs to rest and they must go. Patricia takes Frankie and William downstairs to make them some bread and jam for tea. William babbles on as usual but Patricia and Frankie's thoughts are still upstairs with the precious new addition to their family.

From that moment, Frankie no longer feels lonely and unwanted. She spends the majority of her free time cuddling and helping to care for this tiny being. As Janet grows, the bond between the two girls becomes closer and stronger. Frankie is also glad that Frederick seems to mellow a little and loses his temper less often. For weeks he leaves Frankie alone, but then the night-time visits and invitations to sit on his lap return and increase in frequency. Whenever this happens, Frankie focuses her mind on her little sister's latest skills. She visualises Janet sitting up for the first time, or the day she started to crawl, or the time she spoke her first word. But then it gets worse.

On Sunday mornings, all three children squash into their parents' bed and play with the baby until Joanna decides it's time to change Janet's nappy and prepare her rusks and milk for breakfast. One Sunday, as soon as Joanna leaves the room Frederick rolls over to Frankie while Patricia and William are laughing and giggling on the other side of the bed. He moves himself above Frankie, places his penis between her legs and begins to push rhythmically back and forth. He pushes harder and it really hurts, but she is too scared to object. The pain becomes intense as the strength of his pushing increases. Frankie knows for sure that this isn't an act of love – quite the opposite. Her daddy can't love her and hurt her like this. Why would her own father be doing this to her? Frankie turns her head toward Patricia and William, but they don't notice what's going on and how distressed she is. She forces herself to focus on her happy times playing with Janet, and pretends this isn't happening. As the pain increases she screws up her eyes and bites her bottom lip to stop herself screaming. When her father moves off, her thoughts are so deep inside her own mind that she feels numb. Before Joanna comes back into the room carrying the changed and fed Janet, Frankie slips out of bed and into the bathroom where she fills up the basin and washes herself. The task calms her down and helps her to behave normally for the rest of the day.

That night, as she lays awake in the darkness, she wonders how much longer she can cope with this life. Can it get worse? Today, the pain was as much as she could take. What can she do? If she tells anyone, they won't believe her. If they do believe her, will her father get locked away? Will she and her sisters and brother have to live in an orphanage? Will she be the cause of breaking up her family? When she eventually falls asleep she dreams of being dragged away and put in a workhouse like Oliver Twist. By morning she knows that she must keep her secret no matter what it costs her.

15

A Broken Promise

Frankie age 12

Frankie is excited. Her father has bribed her with the promise of a new dress. She usually has to wear Patricia's hand-me-downs so it really is exciting.

Saturday arrives and the whole family piles into the car to go into town. Frederick parks the car and removes Janet's folding pushchair from the boot. Frankie hops impatiently from one foot to the other while Joanna straps Janet in. They set off towards Marks and Spencer and the nearer they get, the more excited Frankie becomes. She arrives first and peers through the glass swing doors of the store. At either side she sees an army of racks stretching into the distance, all arranged in neat rows and adorned with colourful clothes. The middle aisle consists of quadrangular counters. Smartly dressed shop assistants stand at each counter. If she squints Frankie can see a large sign hanging from the ceiling further back in the store. It is covered in colourful flowers and butterflies, and it proclaims, 'Children's Department'.

At that moment Frederick arrives and pushes the glass door open. He walks through, leaving Joanna to hold the door open as the rest of the family enter. Now begins the adventure that Frankie has been looking forward to. They make their way towards the colourful sign. Frankie grips Patricia's hand, trying to contain her emotions. One day she hopes she might be curvy like Patricia, but today it doesn't matter that she is gawky and has to wear glasses, and that Mummy cuts her fringe all wrong and that her hairgrips don't do anything to improve her hairstyle. Soon she will have a new dress!

Frankie knows Patricia is Daddy's favourite. He doesn't really care about her or William. In fact he always seems angry that William's red hair keeps sticking up even when he tries to wet it down, and he always loses his temper with William even when he's not doing anything naughty. But Patricia is different. Daddy seems pleased when young men glance at Patricia. She's only fifteen, but he likes to show her off.

Suddenly an outfit catches Frederick's eye. It's a bright purple straight skirt with a matching jacket. He holds it up to show Joanna.

"This would look amazing on Pat, don't you think?" he asks.

Joanna feels the purple textured fabric and holds the outfit against Patricia, who drops her sister's hand and turns her full attention to her parents and the purple outfit. Her beautiful face breaks into a smile as her mother says, "Oh yes, it's definitely Pat's colour and style. Let's go and try it on her."

Frankie's excitement fades a little, but her turn will come next. While Joanna and Patricia are in the changing room, she wants to hold William's hand for reassurance, but he shrugs her off. William never seems to be happy at home or at school, or with his sisters. He is always taking his sticky-up red hair off to play football with his mates. Yet he is still a baby really, wetting the bed and needing a rubber sheet, especially when Uncle James visits. Frankie feels sorry for William.

When Patricia and Joanna come out of the changing room Patricia does a twirl in the purple skirt and jacket and her smile shoots pleadingly towards her father. Frederick's eyes light up.

"Well, what do you think?" he asks Joanna.

Joanna nods at her husband and he nods back. Patricia claps her hands in glee. Frankie's hopes rise as she anticipates that she will be the next one to accompany her mother into the changing room. William looks on with an expression of total disinterest. When Joanna and Patricia emerge again with the purple outfit in hand, Frederick takes them to the counter to pay the smiling assistant, who carefully folds and wraps the outfit in pink tissue paper and puts it in the special white, ribbon-handled, Marks and Spencer bag. As Frederick hands the bag to Patricia he has the glint in his eye that Frankie knows so well. Patricia is looking a bit uncomfortable, but now Frankie is looking at a row of bright dresses hanging on a nearby rail.

One dress fascinates her. It is pale blue and it's covered in small white daisies with yellow centres. It's got a white Peter Pan collar and matching turn-ups on each short puffed sleeve. It's got a white shiny belt that buckles at the front, and she can't take her eyes off it. That will be the dress she chooses. It will be like wearing a meadow of flowers.

Then something terrible happens.

"Come on, Frankie," her mother says, "Don't just stand there day dreaming. We need to get back to the car before the parking fee runs out."

"But..."

"Come on, girl!" Frederick says. The family are already walking towards the exit. Yet her dress is in the other direction. Then reality hits her. Her father has forgotten he has promised to buy her a new dress.

She runs to catch up with her family. Patricia takes her hand as if to comfort her. Patricia knows that Frankie should have got a new dress, but if she says anything she will risk losing her own new outfit. She can't bring herself to take that risk, so instead squeezes her younger sister's small bony hand in the hope that this will compensate.

Outside the store, Frederick and Joanna stride forward with the three children struggling to keep up. Pent up emotion overwhelms Frankie, and silent tears run down her hot cheeks to drip from her chin onto her faded cotton dress. Joanna looks behind and sees Frankie's tears.

"What are you crying for now?" she asks brusquely.

"Daddy promised he would buy me a new dress today!" she blurts out, "but instead he bought Pat an outfit and forgot all about me!"

There's a moment of silence in which Frankie imagines Frederick might be feeling guilty. But then he laughs and says, "Okay, so you're jealous, are you? We shall have to buy you something too I suppose or I'll never hear the end of it."

Now Frankie feels guilty for resenting Patricia's enjoyment, and her face burns with shame. She no longer wants a new dress. She wants to curl up, invisible.

"Fine!" says Frederick, "We shall go into this shop right here and buy you a dress!" He turns into a shabby looking store run by an Indian family. Inside there are no bright rows of dresses with flowers on them. Instead there are scouring pads, breakfast cereals, and metal screws, and rolled up rugs, and smelly things to cook with. Frankie sees just one dress on display. It is the ugliest dress she has ever seen. It has big red shapes on a white background, a square neck and no sleeves. At the waist there is a wide belt of the same ugly material. Frankie instantly hates it, but to her astonishment, her father points to the dress and says, "That one will do. It's just right for Frankie isn't it, Joanna?"

"Oh that's really pretty!" agrees Joanna.

Frankie is steered into a curtain-fronted cubicle and given the dress to try on. She struggles into the red and white monstrosity. Shyly she emerges from the cubicle feeling self conscious and ungainly.

"That looks fine!" chorus Frederick and Joanna. They are trying to sound enthusiastic, but Frankie knows they are not. She looks over to her sister and brother for support, thinking, 'Surely they can see how awful it looks!'

Patricia avoids Frankie's pleading gaze, and William looks totally disinterested as usual.

"We'll have that one," announces Frederick to the small grey-haired man behind the till. "Patricia, help Frankie to take it off."

Within five minutes of entering the shop, the family is rushing back to the car. They get there before the parking attendant can give them a ticket. All the way home Frankie is silent, stunned and nauseous on the back seat.

Once home she takes the dreaded dress to her bedroom, and dutifully hangs it in the wardrobe before she climbs up the ladder to her top bunk bed. Then Patricia bursts in. "Let's have a try-on, Frankie!"

Frankie doesn't want to try on her dress and she doesn't want to disappoint her sister and she doesn't know what she wants, but she climbs down and helps Patricia carefully open her parcel from Marks and Spencer.

Naturally Patricia looks gorgeous in her new outfit, and Frankie tells her that the skirt is lovely and the purple really suits her.

"Now it's your turn," Patricia orders, "Let's see you in your new dress."

Frankie obediently slips on the horror from the Indian shop. Patricia zips her up and helps her to do up the buckle on the belt. Both girls stand before the mirror in silence.

"I hate it!" bursts out Frankie as the tears begin all over again.

"Cheer up," says Patricia, "It could be worse."

But it couldn't be worse.

That night, tucked up in her bed above Patricia, with Janet fast asleep in her cot in the opposite corner of the bedroom, Frankie thinks back over her twelve years of life. She tries to think of happy times. She dreams about the Christmas when she was four, when they got their furry Sooty, Sweep and Sue puppets. Frankie still has her Sue puppet, which lives in the toy box in the bottom of the fitted wardrobe. Sometimes she stills get it out for a cuddle. But she knows that even her Sue puppet can't make her new dress beautiful.

— 16 —

The last counselling session

Frankie age 50

Frankie walks slowly into the counsellor's room for the last time. The several dreams and new memories that surfaced during the week have left her exhausted and demotivated. With hunched shoulders and dull eyes she cannot summon up a smile to greet the woman with whom she has become so close.

The counsellor gauges her mood in an instant and touches Frankie's hand.

"As it's our last session, we have an extra half hour to tie up the ends."

Frankie nods.

"I take it you've had a hard week and are rather weary?" the counsellor asks.

Frankie can only nod again.

"Do you feel able to outline what has come to the surface since we last met?"

Frankie takes a deep breath and begins. She relates the summary of her realisations.

"Well, I remembered that my grandmother and grandfather compensated for the lack of love at home. I spent lovely weekends with them, but then they moved away. That

---

broke my heart. It left me without any love and support. I was incredibly sad after that. We occasionally visited Nan and Granddad and I enjoyed those times, but they just made home seem worse.

When my young sister Janet was born it was the happiest day of my life. It started a new era for me. At last I had someone to love unconditionally who also gave me back the same unconditional love. I still had to put up with the abuse but it somehow seemed more bearable with Janet as a distraction."

"I'm curious, Frankie. When and how did the abuse stop?" asks the counsellor.

This question hits Frankie like a steam train. She takes a few seconds to catch her breath. She digs deep for the memory. As the facts seep into her conscious mind the colour drains from her face and feelings of guilt and confusion flood her. She begins hesitantly.

"I was fourteen and at grammar school. All my friends had started their periods. I hadn't. I had no figure to speak of. In the cloakroom they would all play pinging each other's bra straps while I hid in a corner trying to melt into the shadows. I hated my body. My lack of curves was a huge embarrassment to me. There was lots of talk about sex, and several of the girls were clearly sexually active. One actually had to leave school because she got pregnant. I wasn't absolutely clear about how you got pregnant, even though my father's demonstrations should have taught me. I thought couples only had sex to have babies. I think I had subconsciously disconnected the link between the sexual abuse from my father and the risk of pregnancy because it was too horrifying to contemplate. However, from my quiet position in the corner of the cloakroom I learned a lot. In fact I learned enough to make me worry about what my father still did to me. The next time he tried to lure me on to his lap, I somehow plucked up all my courage and quietly but assertively said 'No'. I was shaking like a leaf both outside and in but I'd managed to say it. I was relieved that he didn't immediately fly into a rage. In fact, he didn't argue or get angry at all. From that moment on he never touched me again. One small word was all it took."

The silence in the room is palpable. Frankie's face is burning. She cannot lift her eyes. She sees her intertwined fingers fidgeting busily in her lap.

The counsellor's voice breaks the silence, "Frankie."

"Frankie," the counsellor repeats, "please look at me."

Shards of sound seem to bounce from wall to wall. Frankie feels like a little girl again as she slowly raises her chin. Her eyes look straight into the warmth and empathy of the woman before her. She makes a conscious effort to keep those eyes steady and as she does so, realises that her own embarrassment is dissolving away. She lets out a long sigh and for a few seconds feels at peace. Then the voices in her head start to whisper guilt. The whisper increases in volume until she is forced to cover her ears and screw up her eyes to protect herself. She begins to panic and hyperventilate.

"Frankie, stop!" says the loud, firm voice of the counsellor.

Silence returns as the voices in her head cease. Frankie opens her eyes and lowers her hands. She accepts the glass of water that the counsellor proffers.

"Tell me," commands the counsellor quietly.

Frankie finally brings herself to speak.

"All those years I put up with the abuse when all I had to say was 'No'. Why didn't I do that before? Why did I allow it to continue? It was my own fault. I only had to say one small word. Deep down, I must have wanted it to continue. My father must have sensed it. That's why he continued. I'm no better than a slut!"

Frankie stops for breath. The secret is out. *She* was the cause of her father's actions. She is no better than the girls at school who slept around at every available opportunity. She is dirty and nasty. She hates herself with great vehemence. She is worth nothing. She is a piece of dirt for people to trample underfoot.

"Not only that," she continues, "but in my mind I'd convinced myself that what he had been doing for so long was a demonstration of his love for me. Suddenly it became clear that he'd never loved me at all. If he had, he'd have been upset when I said "No.""

Frankie waits for the firm voice of reason to come from the counsellor. There is silence. She begins to panic again and her thoughts work overtime.

'Oh my God, she is going to agree with all the things I thought about myself! I really am a hateful human being. How am I going to live with myself? What must my kids think of me? Please God help me, help me!' Frankie thinks. Then the counsellor speaks.

"Your father did pretty darn well making you think like that, didn't he, Frankie?"

Frankie looks with wide surprised eyes at the counsellor. "Pardon?"

"Clever man. That's exactly the way abusers work. They put the responsibility fairly and squarely on the victim's shoulders."

"What do you mean?"

"Cowards never take responsibility for their own actions. No doubt he would say that he was doing you a favour. He was opening your mind to pleasures that you were unaware of. He was doing something nice to you, not hurting you. After all, you never stopped him."

Frankie is speechless.

"He was playing with your mind and your emotions, Frankie. It is a well-known behaviour of abusers. He knew you were desperate for love and attention, and he counted on the fact that you'd interpret his actions to be just that. He offered you bribes to do what he wanted. He knew that by accepting those bribes, you would feel responsible for what was happening. But think about who was depriving you of the things you were entitled to in the first place. Your father deprived you of love and attention. He even deprived you of pretty clothes."

Frankie knows she is an intelligent woman. She knows that what the counsellor is saying makes total sense. She knows she would have said the same to anyone else in her position. Suddenly her mind clears. She sees the light at the end of her self-made tunnel.

"You're right. What have I been doing all these years? Why didn't I see all this before? I must be thick!"

The counsellor smiles. "You're not thick, Frankie. It's just that what you learn as a child is really hard to unlearn in adulthood."

"I always knew that in theory but I've never been able to apply it to myself. It's so simple but so hard," Frankie observes. "You've opened my eyes. I don't have to loath myself. You've made me see that I'm an okay person. I've always loved other people, but now I can learn to love myself for the first time in my life."

Frankie feels happiness and laughter bubbling up inside her. She grins. Then starts to giggle. Before she knows it, she is laughing loudly from the very centre of her being. The counsellor catches Frankie's happiness and is soon laughing with her. Spontaneously they stand and hug until they both calm down. Then they separate, slightly embarrassed and awkward.

"I don't know how to thank you enough," says Frankie warmly.

"I'm just happy that you've found your way to this point. You've shown courage and resolve. I'm proud of you, Frankie."

The counsellor hesitates before proceeding.

"I don't want to pour cold water on your joy, but I feel I must warn you that it's probably not going to be a bed of roses for you from here on out."

Frankie looks at the counsellor enquiringly.

"You don't unlearn in six one-hour sessions what you learned over many years. I suspect that all sorts of thoughts and new memories will come up over the next several months, if not years. You may not find those easy to resolve. It is not unusual for a person to need several sessions of counselling over the course of time. But you've taken a huge stride forward, Frankie, and I wish you well in your life and your new career."

Frankie shakes the hand of the woman that guided her through the ups and downs of the last six weeks. She is quite emotional at the thought of not seeing the counsellor again, and can't trust herself to say anything. She leaves the room for the last time, with head held high and a bounce in her step. She will move forward into her future. She is still wondering what that future will hold when she arrives in the office to meet life head on.

—17—

Harsh Reality

Frankie age 50

Frankie's blue eyes sparkle. She knows that she is about to start a new era of her life – one that is free from self-loathing and guilt. Today she feels she could take on the world. Nothing can wipe the smile from her face.

She parks her car in her office car park, and keys in the door-code to enter, expecting the usual warm welcome from her colleagues. She stops and looks around. It's only a small office. Each of the six desks has a computer terminal, filing cabinet, and usually its own busy social worker, but today nobody is here. Frankie looks towards the far end where a door leads into the team manager's office. Mostly this door is open but now it's closed. Her sixth sense tells her that all is not well. She heads straight for that office without stopping to dump her belongings. When she looks through the small window in the door she sees her manager and fellow social workers standing in a cluster, coffees in hands, and shocked looks on faces. She knocks. The manager beckons to her to enter. A hush hangs heavy in the room as five sets of glazed eyes turn to look at her. A few of her colleagues have tear-stained cheeks. Something is very wrong.

"Come on in, Frankie," her manager says, as she pours another coffee and offers it to Frankie.

Frankie takes the cup, wondering why Michael, the only male social worker in the team, is not present. Surely Michael should be included if the team has to face something unpalatable. She remembers that he was playing an important football match last night. He's a fit twenty-four year-old but he might have been injured and had to stay home.

"I'm afraid we've just received some bad news," says the manager. Frankie thinks that is already pretty obvious. She takes a large gulp of coffee.

"As you know, Michael was playing in a football match last night." Frankie nods, guessing that her assumption about an injury is correct.

"During the match, he suddenly collapsed, and I'm afraid that he could not be revived."

The words hit Frankie full on but bounce straight back off. She can't absorb what she has just heard. One of her colleagues lets out a small sob. Another sniffs.

The manager approaches and places her arm around her student's shoulders. "Do you understand what I'm saying, Frankie? Michael is dead."

Frankie's mind goes into a swirl. Thoughts rush in, around and out again. Surely someone has made an awful mistake. It can't be true.

"But he's too young and fit to die. It's impossible!" she says.

A team member places a chair behind Frankie and the manager guides her into it. Her head is thumping with the building pressure. She feels faint. One of the social workers crouches down in front of her and holds both of her hands firmly before she says, "I'm afraid it's not a mistake, Frankie. Michael is dead. We are all in shock."

Frankie's voice trembles as she attempts to respond.

"I'm sorry. I feel ashamed of myself. I'm older than most of you and have known Michael for much less time than you, and yet I make a fool of myself. How selfish of me. Please forgive me."

The atmosphere lightens a little, now that everyone knows. The team manager squeezes Frankie's shoulder. Positivity seeps back into the room, and a sense of 'business as usual' prevails.

"Right then," begins the manager, "I'll go through Michael's caseload and re-allocate the individual cases. It will mean us all pulling together for a while to prevent the service to our clients being affected, but I know you'll help out and we'll manage until I can find a temp."

Everyone nods and disperses to their individual workstations to immerse themselves in the day's tasks. They are determined to reclaim a sense of normality. For social workers that means an ever-boiling kettle and a vast array of cakes and biscuits to fuel them. The bustle returns, if a little more subdued than normal.

"Can I have a word with you, please?"

It takes a few seconds for Frankie to realise that the manager's words are directed at her. She picks up her notebook and pen and joins the kindly lady in her office.

"I'm sorry I didn't ask you sooner, but how did your last counselling session go?"

Frankie hasn't thought about the counselling since she got to the office, although earlier she had been radiant with the change she has experienced. She recaptures that feeling as she starts to recount the events of that last session. Excitement re-emerges and bubbles up inside her. A smile appears on the manager's face as Frankie's happiness travels across the space between the two women.

"I've turned a corner," Frankie explains, "With the help of the counsellor, I've learned that being abused wasn't my fault. In fact, I'm an okay person and I'm allowed to like myself."

"I'm really pleased for you. It took great courage to seek help, and even greater courage to face the ghosts of your childhood," she says. "I know that your professional practice will only benefit from this experience as you grow and develop into your role."

Frankie thanks her and is about to rise from her chair and leave the office when her manager continues.

"So, what impact do you think the counselling will have on you as a person and a social worker from now on?"

"Wow that's a big question," retorts Frankie, "I suspect I will need to think long and hard about how the abuse had already affected me and defined my character. Then I can go on to think about the impact the counselling will have on my future behaviour."

"Yes, I believe you're right," says the manager, "I shall look forward to having that question answered by the time we meet for our next session one month from now. That will be our last before you leave, and I'll be able to tell you if you've passed your placement or not."

Frankie reflects on how quickly her time with the Learning Disabilities Team has flown by, and realises she'll have lots of thinking to do in the coming month if she's to be able to provide a good answer and pass her placement. It is a reasonable thing for her manager to expect an understanding of the relationship between her professional role and her insights from counselling.

As Frankie leaves her manager's office, she recalls the words of her counsellor. New memories are still likely to surface. She knows that's exactly what will need to happen to enable her to analyse her own behaviour. She feels stronger and much more resilient than she ever has before, and quite relishes taking up this challenge.

That night Frankie lays in bed beside her husband, Alex, secure in her marriage. From that safe place she starts to dig into her memories as she drifts to sleep. She will identify how the abuse actually did affect her. Her eyes close. She is fifteen again...

— 18 —

Memory #1 - First Love

Frankie age 15

"Do you Like Jack or not?"

Frankie's friend, Julia, a slim, blond haired girl, sits next to her on the bed, waiting for an answer. The friends always get a lift to school from Julia's dad, a northern man from whom Julia has inherited her no nonsense approach. The few minutes they spend together in Julia's bedroom each morning is when they talk about private issues such as their love lives.

"Whose idea is this?" replies Frankie.

"Jack's. You know that my boyfriend, Lenny, is Jack's best friend. Well Jack brought up the subject with Lenny. Lenny asked me if I thought you might like Jack enough to go out with him. I said I'd ask you. Simple!"

It sounds anything but simple to Frankie as she sits beside Julia thinking about the question. Her mind as usual is working overtime. 'Why would anyone want to go out with me?' she thinks, 'I've no figure to speak of, I wear glasses, I'm shy around boys, I'm plain, my hair is mousy and I'm not exactly a fashion icon. And I'm a geek because I go to grammar school.' Having listed all the reasons she can think of, she is certain no boy would actually be interested in her. She is totally non-descript and boring.

"Well, think about it," says Julia as her dad calls up the stairs to tell them it's time to go.

Frankie has her answer by the time she leaves school that evening. It's yes. What is there to lose? She tells Julia as they cut across the common to save their bus fares. Julia is ecstatic.

"That's brilliant, Frankie. We can make a foursome and go to the church youth club together on Wednesday." Frankie catches Julia's sense of excitement as they chatter away happily, not even noticing the long walk.

Time drags until Wednesday, but at last the two girls are making their way towards the church hall, having spent the past hour in Julia's bedroom helping each other with hair and makeup. Frankie is wearing tight blue jeans and a pale blue polar neck sweater that brings out the colour of her eyes. Julia is wearing jeans too but her sweater is cream coloured to match her blond hair. They enter the church hall. Music is blaring in the background as Julia scans the groups of young people drinking coffee, playing snooker, or just standing around chatting. Frankie's heart is thumping so hard that she wonders if everyone can hear it.

"There they are," says Julia. She pulls Frankie by the arm toward Lenny and Jack, who are leaning against the wall chatting to some other guys. Julia walks straight up to Lenny with her friend in tow, and he leans down to plant a quick kiss on her cheek. Jack smiles shyly at Frankie and says hello. It's very hot with so many people crammed into the hall, so the four decide to go outside for some fresh air. They sit on the steps leading to the hall door, and conversation comes easily. As they chat, Jack moves closer to Frankie and takes her hand. She doesn't resist. They glance into each other's eyes and the chemistry between them flares. Conversation continues and the time flies by.

"Hey you two," Julia interrupts. Frankie and Jack jump.

"Lenny is walking me home now, so I'll see you tomorrow morning at my place as usual, Frankie." As Julia and Lenny walk off together, the new couple continue to sit side by side and hand in hand, waving goodbye to their disappearing friends.

"May I walk you home?" asks Jack looking slightly embarrassed.

"Yes please," replies Frankie, knowing her pink cheeks are glowing with anticipation. Jack stands up, pulling Frankie with him and drawing her closer with his other hand. He leans down and kisses her gently. She kisses him back. Fireworks explode in each of their young hearts.

Frankie doesn't remember the walk to her house. She finds herself on the doorstep in Jack's embrace, thinking that her heart is going to burst. Then suddenly, "Get indoors this minute, Young Lady! You're late and your mother's been worried." Her father is standing inside the open front door looking furious. He ignores Jack, pulls his daughter into the hallway by her wrist and slams the door. Frankie yelps with shock and pain. She rubs her sore wrist and runs upstairs to her bedroom and to safety. Her father hasn't sexually abused her for almost a year since she put an end to it when she was fourteen, but he still continues the physical abuse, so she is well aware of his strength when he loses his temper.

The rest of the week is busy for Frankie. She is studying hard for her General Certificate of Education, and despite her father's behaviour on Wednesday evening she is buoyed up with her memory of Jack's kisses. At school on Thursday morning Julia tells Frankie that Lenny rang to arrange another foursome to the cinema on Saturday. Frankie is relieved that Jack wasn't put off by her father's rudeness. She is really excited about seeing him for a second time, and wonders if they will sit in the back row of the cinema - the traditional preference of young courting couples. Her tummy does a flip as she contemplates the idea.

Frankie's parents give her permission to go out, on condition that she is back home and Jack is gone by 10p.m. The second date is a great success, not least because the back seats of the cinema turn out to be every bit as enjoyable as in Frankie's daydreams. The kissing stokes the couple's fervour until their hearts beat so fast that it takes their breath away. When the lights come up, the four friends realise that they've been so focussed on their partners that they've missed most of the film, but the rosy cheeks of both girls confirm the unimportance of that fact. Frankie arrives home with time for a last kiss from Jack in the hallway of her house before she hears her mother's shout.

"It's ten o'clock."

Jack leaves hastily.

Frankie's elation doesn't last long. The next morning, she finds herself once more at the end of her father's temper. He attacks her with greater ferocity than ever before and destroys her most loved glass animals. Yet despite the beatings she continues to be happy with Jack.

Over the course of the next few months, Jack somehow manages to endear himself to Frankie's parents, and they invite him to stay with them for the weekend in their holiday chalet at the seaside. This is the first year that Patricia won't be with them on holiday, because now she's married to Anton, but Jack will be, and Frankie is thrilled. She sits in the chalet with her parents waiting for Jack to arrive on his motorbike.

That first night, Jack sleeps on a fold-up bed in the bay window of the small lounge, with William on the sofa. Frankie sleeps on the top bunk bed in the small bedroom, with Janet down below. Joanna and Frederick have the larger room.

The next morning, young Janet is up and playing outside early. Jack comes to Frankie's room and wakes Frankie with a tender kiss. He leaves to get dressed after just one minute. Frankie is contemplating getting up when Joanna enters the bedroom looking serious.

"I just saw Jack leave your room. What have you two been up to?" she asks in a loud whisper, "Did Jack touch you? I saw him leave your room and go straight to the kitchen sink to wash his hands."

Frankie is disgusted with her mother's crude words, and shocked to the core. Her mother has never protected her from her father. How dare she make such comments! She has no right to be so 'high and mighty'. Joanna's question is left unanswered as Frankie pushes back her covers and climbs down the ladder to the floor, blanking her mother completely.

Later that day, she and Jack go for a walk up to the cliff top to get away from Frankie's parents. They lay beside each other on the grass, enjoying the warm rays of sunshine. Jack strokes Frankie's leg as they talk, totally immersed in each other. Frankie is very aware of the warmth of Jack's fingers, and isn't totally surprised when he turns to look into her eyes. She sees a warm question in his gaze. He hesitates, and then his hand gently slides under her skirt and up to the top of her inside thigh. "I really love you, Frankie. Can I just caress you? I won't hurt you, and I promise it will be nice."

Frankie freezes. Her body longs for his touch but her thoughts take her straight back to her father's abuse, and a battle commences inside her mind. She knows this is the way to show a man you love him. If she says no he might ditch her. But is it right? Will he think I'm a slut if I let him do this? She is still struggling with her inner dilemma when Jack takes her silence as consent, and his hand begins to press and caress her pubic bone, and his fingers creep under her panties. She desires him, but she is numb, and can't feel what he wants.

Over the next few weeks the petting gets more and more intense and Frankie finds herself slowly relaxing and enjoying. One day Jack unzips, and Frankie lies back and it is done. Frankie knows this is proof that Jack loves her. She forgets that once she thought her father loved her too, although he hurt her so.

They do not take precautions simply because they are too embarrassed to go to the chemist shop and ask for what they need. And they are lucky. Over the next year they become closer, their relationship stronger. Each cannot imagine being without the other. Frankie's parents like Jack. He is just the person to eventually take Frankie off their hands.

Frankie leaves school when she reaches sixteen, and starts work in a research laboratory. She is one young female in a predominantly male environment. Her teammates are all married with families of their own, and they take Frankie under their wing and invite her to several social events. The workplace atmosphere is warm and relaxed, and Frankie is very happy there. The guys constantly play jokes on her, like creeping up behind her while she is busy writing reports at her desk, and tying the loose ends of her lab coat belt to the back of her chair. Then they stand at the far end of the laboratory and call her, laughing hysterically when she stands up and drags the chair along behind her. She is not fazed by this and enjoys being the happy centre of attention, something she never is at home. Soon some of the younger guys begin to notice her. She enjoys this and doesn't take is seriously, but it does force her to think about Jack. Eventually she realises that she no longer loves him the way she did. He was her first, but she now knows that it is over for her.

When she tells Jack he is devastated.

———

Joanna and Frederick don't accept her decision. They are still convinced that Jack is the young man to take on the responsibility of Frankie. After two weeks of pressure from her parents, and not being able to stand the look of misery on Jack's face, she relents. She will never truly escape from the control of her father, and now she is stuck in a relationship she feels she cannot get out of. She and Jack continue. She has not steered her own life as she wanted to. She makes the best of it.

The relationship drags on until, on the hottest day of the year, the couple eventually marry three months before her twentieth birthday. Their friends Anita and Alex are bridesmaid and Best Man. When Alex hugs her before she leaves for her honeymoon, Frankie responds with more warmth than she ever feels when Jack embraces her. She is surprised by that, but ignores the fact and sets out with her new husband, hoping that everything will come right with her and Jack in the course of time.

They return from the honeymoon to married life as if they were an older couple, blunted by familiarity. Life continues. They regularly visit their parents at weekends, and also Patricia and Anton who now live in the countryside. Janet pops in from time to time, which both Frankie and Jack enjoy. They continue to be regular churchgoers and become involved in church youth work. There is no longer any excitement in life, but Frankie learns to accept that.

They agree it's time to try for a baby and are content with the decision. When Frankie is still not pregnant several months later she begins to wonder if they will ever succeed. She feels desperate with worry.

Jack spends more and more hours working at his father's building and decorating business. Frankie also has to cope with constant nastiness and bullying from her mother-in-law. Jack's mother loves to put her in embarrassing positions in an attempt to show her up. She even insists that when they go there to tea, they must not eat their potato crisps with their fingers but with their knives and forks. Jack ignores this but Frankie feels so threatened by this woman that she does her best to balance the crisps on her fork whilst the wicked witch of the west (Frankie's secret nickname for her) watches on with a satisfied smirk on her superior face.

Frankie feels that she's just swapped one bully for another. She has left her father but she is now landed with her mother-in-law. She understands why her father-in-law spends so much time at work. He would want to be away from his dragon of a wife as much as possible. Jack and his father really do need to work hard but Frankie feels disappointed that Jack doesn't seem to want to spend more time with her, and above all she feels very lonely. Jack's mother is jealous of her, and she sees Jack's inability to confront his mother, to stand up for his wife, as a real weakness. He seems to be totally unaware of Frankie's needs. She tries and tries to distract herself by concentrating on her job, but eventually she concedes that, for her, the marriage is at breaking point. She realises that she feels as unhappy as she did when she lived with her parents, and often daydreams about running away. Sometimes when she's feeling really low, she thinks that she'd be better off dead, but she knows that she'd never find the courage to take her own life.

She drags herself to work each morning, finding comfort in the fact that she can at least lose herself in her research projects, but she seriously wonders how much longer she can go on living her life like this.

She wonders if she could face the shame of getting a divorce, especially the judgement of those within the church. She decides to give herself one more month to think about it, after which she will definitely decide what to do.

— 19 —

Memory #2 -The First Affair

Frankie aged 21

Frankie is still feeling very low, when one day she finds herself gravitating towards a work colleague called Ralph. She has had little to do with him before, but now she has begun to notice him.

Ralph is tall, well built and in his early 40s. He has the body of a rugby player and a sparkle in his eyes whenever he comes into the laboratory where Frankie works. He is the Factory Manager, and she doesn't really know why he is affecting her now, because he's been walking around the place for years.

Some of the equipment used by the laboratory is shared with and located in the Works Office where Ralph's team sits. As part of her work developing new alloys for use as bearings in Rolls Royce aeroplane engines, Frankie often uses the test equipment located in the Works Office. The guys in the Works Office are different to those in the Research Laboratory, more direct in their admiration of her and her mini skirts. When she enters the Works Office there are always wolf whistles. In the laboratory the guys call her Twiggy, after the model, and chat quite a bit. In the Works Office, they just whistle, but eventually she realises they are a friendly and welcoming group to work alongside. As Manager, Ralph has his own office, but he comes in often to speak to his men, and frequently stops to talk and laugh with Frankie when she's working in there. Frankie's confidence gradually increases.

One particular day, Ralph spends a lot of time asking her about her research projects. He is interested because he will be in charge of the future production process of the alloys she's developing. But there is something else happening. Ralph has a way of looking intently into her eyes as he talks with her, and she finds herself responding. He invites her into his office to discuss the project further, away from the busyness of the Works Office.

The discussions in Ralph's office become more regular, and soon a strong chemistry develops between them. Soon Ralph asks Frankie to meet him on her Friday afternoon off. The invitation is irresistible.

They meet outside a well-known concert hall in a local town. Frankie travels there by bus, and Ralph picks her up in his car. They drive into the countryside; find a hillside overlooking a golf course, and sit chatting in the sun. When Ralph bends to kiss her Frankie can hardly breathe. Their want and need of each other rises until their bodies become entwined in slow and sensuous completion.

Frankie loses her heart to Ralph as they become one on that hillside on that first Friday afternoon. Ralph has a wife, and Frankie has a husband, but those facts are irrelevant as they lay there floating in the aftermath of lovemaking. Frankie knows with certainty that this will be the first of many Friday afternoons together.

The trip home on the bus is uncomfortable because Frankie feels that everyone at the bus stop is staring knowingly at her. She is still flushed and is sure that her high colour gives her away. They must know she is an adulteress.

Her feelings of guilt and shame transport her back to her childhood and how she felt after sexual encounters with her father. She hates herself for what she's just done. She wonders how she will ever be able to hide it from Jack. By the time she arrives at her front door she's telling herself that she will never do it again. Yet a small voice deep inside tells her she will.

Once inside the flat, Frankie runs a bath and relaxes in the warm glow. She looks down at her body, which she feels sure must have changed after such a fulfilling experience. Her nipples stand erect as she thinks about Ralph and the intensity of her attraction to him. She closes her eyes and relives the experience on the hillside overlooking the golf course. Her body throbs with renewed sexual hunger. If Ralph were here with her now, they would both be eager to repeat their lovemaking.

As the bath water cools, Frankie realises she should have used some form of contraception. She and Jack never use anything and she still hasn't got pregnant, but she makes a conscious decision to always make love with Jack on a Friday night so that, should the unthinkable happen, she can always choose to believe that Jack is the father. These are the ways an adulteress thinks.

Frankie is so besotted with Ralph that she daydreams about him at every available opportunity. As she and Jack are driving somewhere in the car, she closes her eyes and dreams about him. As she sits in front of the television each evening, her mind is elsewhere. Even as she sits in boring church meetings, she relives her times with the man she now loves, and is grateful that nobody can see into her mind. She believes in God but it doesn't occur to her that God knows her every thought. She exists by living a parallel dream life.

She acts out her mundane life like a puppet, whilst losing herself in her happy thoughts.

Life is now bearable for Frankie. She spends as much time at work and with Ralph as she can. She lives for Friday afternoons and the love, affection and sexual adventures they bring. She no longer minds that Jack works long hours. Any time she spends alone serves as daydreaming time.

She still enjoys being woken by Jack each morning with a cup of tea in his hand, but now she loves to spend hours getting herself ready for work, which entails making herself as attractive as possible. She always has a reason for buying new clothes, not because she needs them, but because they attract compliments from her secret lover.

On arrival at work each morning, her first task is to open her diary to remind herself what the day holds in store. This Monday morning she notices a small black star at the top right-hand corner of the page. A star is Frankie's code to remind her to expect her period to begin. She hates seeing the star as it means that her Friday afternoon activities are likely to be curtailed.

A few work colleagues walk into the office chatting about their weekend activities. They pause just long enough to say good morning and gesture their need for coffee. Frankie fills the electric kettle with fresh water and brings it to the boil. She spoons the Nescafe into the mugs, pours in the boiling water, and adds the milk from the carton brought in by one of her team mates. Usually, Ralph appears just as she is handing the filled coffee cups around, but today he doesn't arrive. 'He must be busy,' thinks Frankie as she finishes drinking her coffee.

Soon, the routine of the day begins. Frankie loves her job more than ever. The knowledge that she will discover lots of new facts and processes, previously unheard of, excites and motivates her. She looks forward to discussing her findings with Ralph later but for the moment she is engrossed in her current experiment. The morning flies by until one of her work mates breaks her concentration with a reminder that it's time to make their way to the staff dining room. Ralph and a couple of the guys from the Works Office are probably already seated at the long table that they all share, and this thought makes Frankie's heart beat faster. She joins the small queue at the serving hatch. While she waits to collect her pre-ordered lunch, she looks over to the long table. Ralph isn't there. He must be particularly busy today. She collects her lunch, sits down with her jovial colleagues who are already laughing and joking, and doesn't give Ralph another thought until she catches some conversation between two men at the far end of the table.

"Yes, they had to call the ambulance last night because of the pain."

"Do they know the cause yet?"

The first colleague shakes his head and changes the subject.

Frankie's anxiety rises. Are they talking about Ralph? She feels too shy and guilty to question the guys in case this makes them suspicious, so she tries to distract herself by continuing to eat her meal, although her appetite seems to have disappeared. After lunch, she returns to the laboratory, and throws herself into her work for the rest of the day. She feels okay but when Ralph doesn't appear the next day or the following one, she begins to panic. 'Perhaps he's gone away on holiday,' she reasons with herself. Yet she knows this is unlikely; he would have told her. 'Perhaps he's been urgently called away to a customer,' she tries to convince herself.

She still doesn't feel confident enough to ask her teammates if they know what has happened to Ralph. She knows they already turn a blind eye to her regularly disappearing to his office, and she doesn't want to risk them putting two and two together. She is aware that she is probably being over cautious in not asking about him, but they know that Ralph is married just as they know she is, so she feels she can't risk it.

The next Friday afternoon she gets a bus to their meeting place but after an hour of waiting, she gives up and goes home. She doesn't repeat her expedition for a second time. The third and fourth weeks come and go but still no Ralph. Frankie tries to make herself accept that he has decided to break with her and will never be returning. When Monday of week five comes around, she has no expectations of seeing the man she loves. She is becoming used to the slow, heavy ache in her heart. She arrives at work, puts the kettle on, and proceeds to make the coffee. Suddenly she hears that wonderful voice.

"Where's my coffee then, Young Lady?"

She spins round at a dizzying speed to see a pale-faced Ralph standing there with the same old sparkle in his eyes. Her heart flips. She uses all her strength to root herself to the spot when what she really wants to do is to run straight into his arms.

"So, what happened to the Get Well card?" he asks.

He sees the confusion in her wide blue eyes.

"Nobody told you?"

She shakes her head.

"You rotten lot!" he says to the others in the laboratory.

"Oh, didn't you know, Frankie?" says the senior technician.

Ralph explains. "I was carted into hospital with a really bad pain in my gut. It turned out to be a perforated stomach ulcer. I was in hospital for two weeks and then ordered to rest for another two. I'm just about fed up with eating porridge and rice pudding!"

For the first time in four weeks Frankie is happy. Ralph is once more standing near her, wearing the broad grin she loves. With her spirits soaring she hands Ralph a cup of coffee and disappears to the laboratory to get on with her work. Ten minutes later, he is standing close behind her. Nobody else is in the laboratory. She feels his tender kiss on the back of her neck and she trembles.

"Come over to my office soon," Ralph orders in an assertive whisper. "I need to catch up on the progress of your research projects." Frankie grins and watches him all the way to the laboratory door. She wishes she wasn't so diligent or she'd run after him now.

Later in the day, she picks up her files from the laboratory office and walks across the yard. She has become a popular girl with the guys in the foundry so there are lots of good-natured smiles, waves and whistles, which make her feel happy and self-assured. She reaches Ralph's office on the other side of the yard, taps on the door and enters. His desk is located at the far end of the room. Large windows look out onto a wide thoroughfare that separates this building and a more modern office block. Ralph looks up as she enters, smiles broadly and beckons her towards one of the chairs on the opposite side of his desk. Butterflies flit around in her stomach. She sits on the chair, places her files on Ralph's empty desk, and proceeds to remove various reports, which she passes to him to read. He scans the reports very briefly and then looks up.

"I'd rather you gave me a verbal update if you don't mind," he says. Her butterflies flap harder. He looks into Frankie's eyes.

"Okay. I can do that," she says, trying to avoid eye contact so that she can think about what she needs to tell him. She is actually going to report on her projects.

She describes several experiments she completed during Ralph's four-week absence, occasionally leaning across his desk to open one of her reports at a page containing photographic evidence. She is so absorbed in what she is saying that she doesn't notice his eyes have not once moved from her face. She is still in full flow when she looks up to ask him if he has any questions. The intensity of his stare unnerves her and she dwindles into silence. Has he been listening to a word of what she has said? In the silence she returns his stare. The clock on the wall is ticking but for them time stands still.

Suddenly the office door flies open. One of the Works team is shouting.

"Ralph, you're needed urgently in the foundry. There's been an accident!"

The meeting ends without a word as Ralph, the Works Manager, rushes out of the office. Frankie gathers up her reports and replaces them in her files. She leaves the office, her thoughts now purely on the plight of factory workers who might be injured. Entering the laboratory office, she places her files on top of her desk and returns to her work. When she is called to the telephone Ralph assures her that there are no injuries, and asks her if she can meet him on Friday afternoon as usual. Of course she says yes. She hums happily through the rest of the day, her thoughts on Ralph rather than the work she is doing now.

— 20 —

Memory # 3 - The black star

Frankie aged 22

Friday lunchtime has arrived at last. After so many weeks apart Frankie is filled with excitement at the prospect of being with Ralph again. She tidies her desk, checks that she has completed her week's work plan, and glances at her diary to check tasks for next week when she suddenly sees it. At the top right-hand corner of next Monday's page is a black star. She freezes, and tries not to gasp.

A black star means that her period is due.

She looks back in her diary and checks the black star from the previous month. She always ticks the star when her period arrives. There is no tick. She has missed a period.

"What's up, Frankie?" one of her workmates asks, "You've gone a bit pale."

Frankie swallows hard, realising that she has been holding her breath. She draws on all her will power to respond calmly.

"No, I'm fine," she says, smiling to cover her shock. "See you Monday. Have a good weekend."

Frankie runs to catch the bus, trying to focus only on the afternoon's prize. She can't wait to jump into Ralph's car when he picks her up at their meeting place. She longs to feel him close to her, and thinks about this for the whole bus journey. By the time she alights at the end of her journey, she has forgotten her earlier shock, but the image of that black star hovers.

After only a few minutes she sees Ralph's car approaching. Rushing over to the kerb where it has come to a standstill, she opens the passenger door and jumps in just before he re-joins the traffic. When she looks at him desire is obvious in his eyes. They smile. Frankie can feel her face turning pink. Ralph places his hand on hers and keeps it there until he has to change gear. They are silent until they reach their favourite place on the hill overlooking the golf course. The sound of the seat belts unfastening means they have arrived. Ralph holds her hand tightly as he leads her to their place among the shrubs, carrying a blanket and a white plastic carrier bag. Soon the blanket is on the ground and Ralph pulls her down beside him. Placing his hand behind her head, he leans in to brush her lips with his. His kiss becomes demanding.

"I've missed you, lovely Frankie," he whispers. Soon they are both in a state of sexual frenzy. Ralph's eyes are closed as he kisses her and deftly removes her panties. This time, instead of entering her he slides his hand up the inside of her thigh until it comes to rest on her vagina and the sensitive hidden nub above. She is wet with desire, but as his hand begins to caress her she feels the coming of fear. Suddenly and without warning, Frankie freezes. Her whole body tenses.

Ralph opens his eyes in surprise, and seeing the fright in Frankie's eyes, removes his hand and sits up.

"What is it? His voice is shaky with surprise and passion.

She screws up her eyes and tries to find a response. She pushes herself up into a sitting position.

"I'm sorry," she says quietly, "I … it … it's hard for me to tell you."

"That's all right. Take your time. I'm listening."

"I had some difficult times in my childhood."

"Go on," he responds, stroking her arm in encouragement.

"When you touched me, which I very much wanted you to do but … well, it gave me a flashback and my body just took over. I'm so sorry. I just couldn't help it." Frankie looks down at the blanket. Her face is burning with a mixture of desire and embarrassment. She wants their lovemaking to continue but can it?

"I might have put you off," she whispers, lifting her eyes to look into his. He takes her hand and places it on his engorged penis.

"Does it feel like you've put me off?" he asks.

They both grin. "We have strawberries and champagne to celebrate the occasion. It's the first time we've managed to be together for several weeks, so let's forget what just happened and enjoy the moment."

Frankie nods as a sense of relief washes over her.

For the next twenty minutes, the couple enjoy the fresh fruit and bubbly alcohol. They chat and laugh happily as the sun and champagne gradually relaxes them. Frankie drinks several plastic glasses of the bubbly liquid to Ralph's one. He has to drive them home and takes his responsibility seriously. When the snack is finished and Ralph has packed the empty containers into his carrier bag, Frankie is more than ready to continue where they left off.

She lays down on the blanket and Ralph joins her. A few deep kisses later, he enters her and they both enjoy making love until Ralph climaxes. Afterwards, they lay on the ground together holding hands. Ralph's breathing becomes slow and deep as he snoozes in the sun. Frankie wonders if she will ever enjoy love making to the full. She needs to be touched and caressed in order to reach an orgasm, but her father has ruined that for her. Her body goes involuntarily numb as soon as she is touched in that way.

When she gets home, she has her bath as usual, and makes sure that she and Jack have sex that night. She no longer sees the act with her husband as making love. The truth is, she definitely no longer loves Jack.

In the early hours of Saturday morning, Frankie's eyes suddenly fly open. She is floating in the pleasant state of half consciousness when she remembers the black star. Her stomach turns over, and before she knows it, she is at the point of vomiting. She flies from her bed into the bathroom just in time to lean over the toilet and eject the contents of her stomach. She continues to retch loudly even when there's nothing else to come up. The noise wakes Jack who quickly joins her in the bathroom and affectionately holds her hair back from her face until the retching subsides. He sees his wife's white face and leads her to the kitchen where he hands her a glass of cold water, which she sips gratefully.

"I must have eaten something that disagreed with me," says Frankie as the colour slowly returns to her face.

"Go back to bed. I'll make you some toast and tea," offers Jack.

She obeys and feels better once she is laying flat. Soon Jack appears with tea and toast, which she accepts gratefully. They both sit in bed enjoying the meal until Jack gets up to prepare for work. Frankie feels fine for the rest of the day and forgets the episode as she catches up on her chores. It's not until the same thing happens on Sunday and again on Monday morning that she suspects she might be pregnant. Her excitement increases as she looks again at the black star in her diary and confirms that she has already missed one period and the next one is due that day.

By Thursday evening she can't keep it to herself any longer. She tells Jack of her suspicion when he eventually gets home from work that evening and he responds with a big hug. He couldn't be more delighted.

Only in quiet moments does Frankie think about the coincidence of her becoming pregnant just a couple of months after starting a sexual relationship with Ralph. She has been trying, unsuccessfully, with Jack for almost three years. Each time the thought arises, she forces it to the back of her mind. She continues to meet with Ralph for the next two Friday afternoons and their relationship goes from strength to strength. He no longer tries to touch her as he did on the afternoon that she froze, for which she is both grateful and disappointed.

After two more weeks there is still no sign of her period and she has been sick every morning. Frankie decides to go to her doctor. He confirms that she is pregnant but warns her of the higher than normal risk of aborting the foetus in a first pregnancy. He suggests that she keeps it to herself until she misses her third period.

When the third black star sits un-ticked in her diary, she is certain that she is carrying a baby inside her. She and Jack tell family and their friends the good news. Everyone is delighted, including her workmates. Ralph is genuinely pleased for her. Her morning sickness disappears at four months. She feels healthier and happier than ever before. Her sex drive returns with a vengeance, making her times with Ralph even more enjoyable. One Friday afternoon, more out of guilt than anything, she tries to indicate to Ralph that the baby could be his. He quickly changes the subject, so she never brings it up again. She expects nothing of the man she loves. Several weeks later he tells her that his wife is pregnant, adding that he doesn't want her to think he's just been 'sowing his wild oats'. She is unfazed at this information. Her love for him is unconditional.

Eventually Frankie's last day at work arrives. She expects to return from maternity leave when her baby is six months old, but she knows that one thing has to end forever. If her baby is to have the best chance of growing up in a happy home, she must finish her affair with Ralph. She doesn't tell him, but her determination is immoveable. She has no doubts. They will never again hold each other or make love together. As she leaves work for the last time, laden with gifts for the baby, her heart rips in two. She cannot stem the tears during her bus journey home and throughout the entire weekend. Jack thinks she's crying because she'll miss work. In reality she's grieving for love found and lost. For the moment, her excitement about the approaching birth is placed on hold. The black cloud hanging over her remains for several days until one morning she wakes up to what feels like a new dawn. She promises herself that from now on she'll only look forward. She has no idea how she will feel when her baby is born, especially if it looks like Ralph, but she puts that thought on the back boiler to be dealt with if and when it happens.

—21—

Memory # 4 - A new mum

Frankie aged 23

"Do not push!" shouts the midwife, "Can you hear me, Frankie? Pant, pant!"

"I can't stop!" Frankie screams at the midwife.

She has been in labour for twelve hours, her blood pressure has hit the ceiling rendering her temporarily blind, and she is no longer in control. Her body is going to eject the cause of her excruciating pain come what may. Jack's hand and arm are badly bruised from her iron grip and he is near to tears with worry about his wife and baby. Frankie doesn't know it, but there are several nurses and doctors in the delivery room who are also worried about their patient and her baby. Suddenly her body gives the biggest push yet, she feels the baby catapult out of her and hears a voice yell, "I've got it. It's all right, I've caught it!"

She hears Jack crying loudly, but she can't hear the baby cry.

"Oh my God, oh my God, it isn't crying. My baby isn't crying!" she gasps.

Time seems to stand still for the new mum. She can hear lots of movement but nobody is telling her what's happening.

Jack is still holding her hand tightly and she can feel his sobs vibrating up her arm.

"Jack, Jack, please tell me what is happening," Frankie begs.

Then she hears it. First a gurgling gasp and then a loud high pitched cry. All at once there is a cheer. Everyone is congratulating Jack, and each other. Frankie feels invisible. But she is so exhausted she really doesn't care, and starts to fall into a deep sleep. Suddenly a warm, soft parcel is plonked across her chest.

"She's beautiful," says Jack, giving Frankie a tender kiss on the lips. "Well done, Darling."

Frankie slips into oblivion. When she wakes she is in a six-bed ward. Her sight has returned and she immediately sees that every bed but hers has a clear plastic cradle next to it. Frankie panics.

"Is my baby dead?"

A nurse appears at her side as if by a miracle.

"No, Frankie. Your baby is alive and well but both you and she need rest to recover from your ordeal."

"How much does she weigh? What colour are her eyes? Does she have any hair? Where is she?"

"Slow down young woman or your blood pressure will go up again," shushes the nurse. "You will see her soon enough. Meanwhile you must get some rest."

When the nurse has left Frankie looks around at the other mums, all of whom are feeding their babies. She feels left out and bereft. 'Why didn't she answer my questions?' Frankie thinks to herself, starting to panic all over again. 'Was she lying? Is there something wrong with my baby? Is she deformed? Oh my God, where is she?' Frankie is convinced they are keeping something from her in case her blood pressure goes up.

It's starting to get dark, yet Frankie recalls someone saying that the time of birth was 7a.m. She must have slept all day. The same nurse returns to her bedside with a sandwich and a cup of tea.

"You missed breakfast, lunch and dinner I'm afraid. All I can offer you is this snack for now. I'm sorry." Frankie accepts the sandwich gratefully. She doesn't realise how hungry she is until she starts to eat it. After a few sips of tea she lies back down and is soon fast asleep again.

She is awoken by the clatter of the doors and the appearance of several cradles being pushed supermarket trolley style into the ward. Each is filled with a crying baby.

Her spirits rise in anticipation at the unique and lovely smell of new born babies and the prospect of seeing her new daughter for the first time. She waits as babies are handed out like prizes, to every one but her. She is now convinced that her baby is at the least ill and possibly even dead. She is in a blind panic by the time the nurse reaches Frankie's bed.

"Where's my baby?" Frankie is utterly bereft.

"Not yet, Frankie," says the nurse sympathetically, "The doctor ordered 36 hours bed rest. We will bring her to you later today."

"But not seeing her is making me more stressed than if you just wheeled her in next to me," Frankie pleads.

"We have to do what the doctor tells us, young woman, so you'll just have to be patient for a bit longer."

She can't eat her breakfast for worrying about her daughter – not that the thick, slimy grey porridge they serve floating in cold milk is particularly appetising anyway. She is uncomfortable sitting in bed because of the many stitches she has had as a result of failing to pant instead of pushing. Her guilt over this, and her misery at being kept from her baby, brings tears. She sits and sobs quietly, wondering how anyone in their right mind could think that giving birth is a happy event. It's no wonder her mother looked so miserable all those years ago when she told her, Patricia and William that she was expecting Janet. She knew something that Frankie is only just finding out.

After lunch and afternoon tea, when Frankie is lying on her side facing away from the door, there is the sound of the nurse backing through the door pulling a cradle behind her. The rattle stops at Frankie's bed.

"Come on then mum. Baby's here and waiting for her feed," chirps the nurse.

'At last!' thinks Frankie. She rolls over and sits up in one move. The nurse places the baby in Frankie's arms. Frankie peers at the little face with its huge blue eyes, button nose and rosebud lips. She waits, but nothing happens. There is no rush of love, no instant recognition, no motherly joy. She peers at the baby's face again. She can only think of the indescribable pain that this little bundle caused. She doesn't recognise it as her own daughter. 'Surely this can't be the child that's been living inside me for nine months,' she thinks. She seriously suspects that the nurse has brought her the wrong baby from the nursery but dares not ask.

Without permission, the nurse undoes the buttons down the front of Frankie's nightdress and pushes the baby to her breast. Then the nurse is pinching her nipple and pushing it into the baby's mouth. Frankie yelps as the little mouth clamps shut, its gums seizing her. The baby opens its mouth wide with fright and lets out a distressed cry.

"Now look what you've done! You've scared your baby," scolds the nurse. Feeling like a school child, Frankie grits her teeth as the nurse repeats her pinching action and the baby repeats its clamping action. Then the tiny little creature proceeds to suck with such strength that the pain shoots from her nipple, through her breast and right down to her toes.

"Fuck, fuck, fuck!" says Frankie under her breath as each suck brings another pain. 'Is there no end to the pain this baby inflicts on me?' she thinks.

"Right. Ten minutes each side, and wind her in between," commands the nurse, who used to be kind but who has now become a uniformed tyrant. The young woman in the adjacent bed looks over at Frankie as the nurse leaves the ward.

"She who must be obeyed!" says the young woman in a fake accent as she giggles conspiratorially. Frankie manages a giggle in response; trying not to grimace at the piercing pain she is experiencing. She looks back down at the baby. This time she checks the tiny fingers and toes. All present and correct. She still feels nothing except guilt for feeling nothing. The only likeness she can see in the baby's face is that of her father. She decides she doesn't even like this baby. Her guilt gets worse. She knows she'll have to put on an act for Jack and her relatives when they visit, and the thought depresses her.

With each passing day Frankie's depression intensifies. The only way she can cope with the feeds and the sight of her child is to sing quietly to it throughout feeding times. The ward orderly thinks this is a show of love for her baby and regularly brings her a bottle of milk to drink while she is feeding. Frankie knows it is not love and that she is a fraud. Her guilt deepens.

Things are no better when she goes home. Her breasts are hard and painful due to the amount of milk her body produces. She only has to think about the baby and milk leaks from her, making large wet patches on her clothes. She feels like a cow. She constantly smells of stale breast milk, which makes her nauseous. When she puts the infant to her breast, sometimes the milk squirts from her with such force that it could hit the opposite wall of the small nursery. The baby has no need to suck. She chokes as the squirting milk hits the back of her throat. She becomes agitated and angry, wriggling and screaming intermittently throughout her feed. This gives her colic, so she cries most of the day.

Frankie's depression deepens until she can only sit with the baby in her arms, crying with it. She still feels no love for her tiny daughter. She worries that the baby will not thrive because of her failure to love her and feed her properly. Eventually her mother, who is getting fed up with popping into the flat each morning to find her daughter and granddaughter in such a distressed state, almost drags Frankie to the doctor. The doctor says that the baby is fine but its mother isn't. He advises she changes to bottle-feeding, adding a little thickener to the formula to prevent the baby's colic. He gives Frankie a couple of pills to dry up her milk. She returns from the surgery feeling much more relaxed. Now all she has to overcome is her dislike of the baby.

Over the next week the tiny girl settles down and her colic disappears, but Frankie's depression remains. Each day she dutifully carries out the duties of a new mum, making sure the baby is bathed, changed and fed at the required times. Between her duties, she puts her baby in its pram outside the front door, ostensibly to give it fresh air but in reality hoping that someone will come and take the baby away. Her baby doesn't get stolen. Her guilt and depression get worse.

One day while the baby, now six weeks old, is sleeping, there is a knock at the door. When Frankie opens it, Ralph is standing on the doorstep. He is the last person she expects to see.

"Well aren't you going to invite me in?" He has that same broad grin on his face.

Frankie is half pleased and half horrified to see him. Good manners make her invite him in as she lifts the sleeping baby from its pram. Ralph looks at the tiny girl in its mother's arms. "She's gorgeous," he says. His face then becomes serious. "I miss you, Frankie. I really do. I would very much like to see you again if you will have me."

"I can't Ralph. I have to think of what's best for my baby now. I would feel guilty if I didn't give her my full attention. I'm sorry," she dwindles to the end of this little speech. By the time she's finished speaking she also knows that love for Ralph has faded and she has no desire to rekindle their relationship.

"Are you sure?" he asks.

"Very sure," she says.

He turns and leaves, and with hunched shoulders steps out into the street.

From that moment, Frankie begins to feel better, her depression lifting. She feels a spark of affection for her daughter, who she and Jack have named Torrin. Frankie starts thinking of Torrin as Torrin, not 'the baby'. Gradually the spark ignites and fills her heart with love for the little girl. But love doesn't help her understand how to deal with her daughter, who is feisty and extremely strong willed. Frankie never experienced good parenting when she was a child, so is at a complete loss when it comes to parenting her own child. The health visitor says only that Torrin is clearly a very intelligent child and will go far, but that is no help to a floundering mum. Frankie decides that all she can do is to give Torrin lots of attention. By the time the little girl is eight months old, her attention span is very short, and by the end of each day Frankie is exhausted.

Frankie misses her work. She occasionally takes her daughter to visit her friends in the laboratory office, but when her manager, having patiently waited for her to be ready to return to work, asks her if she will be coming back, she declines. Seeing Ralph again reminds Frankie of her pledge to keep away from him. She thinks back to the exciting months of their affair and how she felt so vital and alive. Now she sees only a dull and loveless life ahead of her again, but she decides to survive by being optimistic. She thinks about all the friends she has, especially Anita and Alex, with whom her and Jack are particularly close. She thinks about her active social life with its many parties.

"Nah! Things are good," she says, trying to convince herself as she gets the bus home from the laboratory with Torrin, "Not exciting, but good."

Despite these determined efforts at being content, Frankie knows that, apart from Torrin, her life is loveless. She remembers how she felt before her affair with Ralph, when she was contemplating taking her own life. She seriously wonders how she can continue. She dares not think too much about the future.

— 22 —

Memory # 5 - A new affair

Frankie aged 26

"This is definitely the one!" exclaims Frankie with a look of pleasure and relief on her face.

Frankie has managed to settle down over the last three years, and she and Jack have already looked at several houses. This one is grubby and needs updating, and the purchase will not be straightforward as the owner is currently ill in hospital, but all of that feels irrelevant. The house feels right, and to Frankie and Jack that is the important thing. Frankie is also pleased that if they buy this house they will be living further away from Jack's bullying mother.

Their negotiations succeed and they eventually move into the house. Frankie hopes that Jack might now start to spend more time at home, especially with all the decorating to do. But he doesn't. Jack still works long hours with his dad. Most of the decorating is done at weekends, and Frankie relies more and more on her parents to look after Torrin, pushing the memories of her abuse so far back in her mind that she's forgotten it ever happened. The thought that she is failing to safeguard her daughter doesn't enter her head.

Torrin continues to be strong-willed. Before she reaches the age of three, she gets thrown out of the church crèche for hitting another child because, in her own words, she "wanted to see what the little girl would do." At a coffee morning, whilst all the children are playing in her bedroom together, she instructs them to remove their clothes before she leads them downstairs with the aim of shocking all the mums. She succeeds, but fortunately Frankie's best friend, Anita, manages to diffuse the situation. Anita, married to Alex, has charisma. Although she doesn't have any children herself, she seems to know how to deal with a bunch of naked small people. She pretends to auction off each child's clothes until all are returned safely to their owners.

Anita, Alex, Frankie and Jack belong to the same church, are active Christians, and are deeply involved in the youth work there. Every Sunday after evening service the four friends get together at Frankie and Jack's house. They enjoy each other's company and they always allow Torrin to stay up to see her favourite 'aunty' and 'uncle'. Anita loves to tell Torrin a bedtime story, and Alex enjoys play fighting with her. Alex and Torrin have a good-natured love-hate relationship. If Torrin kicks or smacks Alex, he kicks or smacks her back. Alex is stronger than Torrin but she will never submit – even if the kick or smack hurts. She is, more than ever, a very determined child.

Frankie is secretly aggravated with Alex. He is tall and handsome with strawberry blond curls, but he has an annoying way of being arrogant. He behaves as if he's the world's expert on everything there is to know. Frankie has a much closer relationship with Anita, but Alex comes with Anita.

Often the two couples arrange to meet up during the week. Because Jack is often late home from work, and Anita is often at the Church Minister's house helping him with a project, Alex and Frankie spend many hours alone together waiting for their partners to arrive. Frankie begins to see that she is not so bothered by Alex's arrogance. It's actually quite attractive, and his blonde curls are cute. Frankie doesn't know if Alex is attracted to her but she senses that he might be. Frankie knows that Alex was not Anita's first choice. Anita once told her in confidence that she had wanted to marry the minister, but he turned her down so she married Alex on the rebound. Sex between Anita and Alex has never been any good apparently, and Anita thinks she might be frigid. This is a great confidence, and Frankie tells nobody about it, but somehow Frankie thinks this makes Alex fair game. Just lately Frankie is feeling restless again, and if Anita doesn't want Alex, then what would be the harm?

One Sunday evening it's Frankie's turn to go to the church service while Jack stays with Torrin. Alex walks Frankie back to her house afterwards. Anita is involved in other activities that night. It's a long walk, so they take the short cut through the cemetery that runs alongside the common. They chat as they walk along the dark pathway, but after a while their conversation dries up. Frankie looks up at six foot two Alex and discovers that he is staring at her. They stop walking. Alex stoops down and kisses Frankie gently on the lips. She responds and the kiss deepens. After a few minutes they pull back from each other. Both feel shocked and embarrassed at what they just did. They know it is not acceptable behaviour for two active church members who are each married to other people. Alex, Anita, Frankie and Jack have all been publically baptised as born-again Christians. Born-again Christians do not commit adultery with their friend's spouse. They walk on in silence.

Back at Frankie's house Jack goes off to prepare a snack supper, and when Anita arrives in her car she takes Torrin up to bed. Frankie and Alex look at each other, feeling the attraction. The air hums between them. Frankie is hungry for excitement and love, and Alex for a woman's body. Frankie already had one affair with Ralph before Torrin was born, somehow disassociating herself from her Christian beliefs at the time. How can she even consider repeating her mistake a second time?

Torrin starts school when she is five years old, which gives Frankie several hours at home alone each day. Alex's job is flexible and he can come and go as he wishes. He starts to telephone Frankie regularly. This develops into visits to Frankie and Jack's house while Jack is at work and Torrin at school. They start a sexual relationship, often making love in Frankie and Jack's bed. It is something they seem to be able to separate from the rest of their lives and from their church beliefs.

Because of Alex, love and excitement return to Frankie's life. Their arrangements work well for two years. Anita doesn't notice as she's too occupied with the church minister, and neither does Jack who still works long hours. As the affair continues, their attraction becomes love. Frankie has become so used to having sex with Jack without use of contraception that it doesn't occur to her to act differently with Alex.

Meanwhile, Frankie's control over six-year-old Torrin is slipping. Torrin wants to walk to school on her own but Frankie refuses to let her. The child persists, continually labouring the point until her mother gives in through sheer lack of energy. Every morning she kisses Torrin goodbye and watches her walk proudly up the road. Once she has turned the corner, Frankie rushes to catch up with her, staying just far enough behind not to be seen among all the other mums and their children walking in the same direction. As soon as Torrin is safely through the school gate, Frankie returns home, feeling like a weird woman who stalks her own daughter. This practice continues until Frankie learns to drive and gets a small car, which encourages Torrin to have a lift instead.

Frankie and Alex cannot keep away from each other. The visits increase and the lovemaking becomes more urgent until eventually the inevitable happens. Frankie gets pregnant. Because of the timing, she knows that Alex is the father. The couple are shocked and full of guilt. Their secret will now be split wide open, and they don't know what to do. They realise what hypocrites they have been, and it dawns on them what a negative influence this will have on the young people with whom they work at church. They also wonder why neither of them had ever thought about contraception. It was so stupid not to. Alex has recently become a church deacon and feels ashamed that he has let down the whole church community. It is the church to whom they now must turn.

"Let's seek advice from Reverend Jones," Alex suggests.

Reverend Jones looked after the church in the interval between the death of the previous minister and the arrival of the new one. Alex makes an appointment for them to visit him at home while Torrin is at school and Jack at work. Reverend Jones is certain what they must do.

"You must each confess to your partner. Find out if Jack is willing to bring up Alex's baby as his own. If not, then Anita might be willing to take on the baby, especially as she is childless. Above all, you must stop seeing each other."

This advice horrifies Frankie. Does he really think she would give up her baby? If she can't have Alex, then she will at least have part of him as compensation. Two sad young people leave the Reverend's house that afternoon. Frankie weeps at the prospect of them living without each other, and worse, how they will cope seeing each other in church and behaving as if nothing is wrong? They have not only lost each other, but also the friendship between the two couples. There'll be no more enjoyable evenings together, and Torrin will miss her auntie and uncle badly. What explanation will Frankie give her? She will not be easily satisfied. The final

goodbye kiss is heartrending for both Frankie and Alex.
Their tears mingle as they hold each other for the last time.

That day Frankie meets her daughter from school
in a state of numbness. To her relief, Torrin doesn't notice
anything strange, and chats away happily all the way home.
For once, Frankie does not argue with her daughter when
she asks for sweets. She takes Torrin to the park and sits on
a bench watching her on the swings and slide, still feeling
nothing.

Jack arrives home later than usual that evening. Torrin
is already in bed. Jack runs upstairs to kiss his daughter
goodnight while Frankie dishes up their dinner. They sit
down to eat together in silence.

"You're unusually quiet this evening," says Jack. "I'm
used to you talking non stop about your day. Is something
wrong?"

Frankie's mouth goes dry. She struggles to swallow her
half-chewed mouthful of food. Her emotions start to get the
upper hand of her and tears begin to form in the corners of
her eyes. She looks down at her plate of food to hide the tears
from Jack but when they plop onto her plate, he can't fail to
notice.

"Frankie, you're starting to frighten me," he says in
alarm. "Are you ill? Is there something wrong with Torrin?
Please tell me."

Frankie looks up and into the eyes of her worried
husband. "Jack, I'm so sorry. There's no easy way to tell you
this but … but …"

"Darling, you know you can tell me anything. Whatever
it is we can deal with it together. Just please tell me."

When Jack reaches across the table and places his hand
over hers Frankie instantly withdraws hers. Tears stream
down her face. Jack takes his handkerchief out of his pocket,
leans over and gently wipes her tears away. His kindness

makes it even more difficult for Frankie to say the words that she knows will hit him like an express train. She can't bear to inflict such hurt on the man that has never been anything but kind to her.

"I have to tell you something that I know is going to hurt you more than I can imagine, but I have no choice and I can only beg your forgiveness."

"Forgiveness? Surely you know I will forgive you anything, Frankie, I love you. You know I do."

"I know, but I also know that I don't deserve you and I certainly don't deserve to be forgiven. I will understand completely if you decide to chuck me out of the house and never want to see me again."

Jack goes pale. "Frankie, that's enough. Just tell me and be done with it."

"I'm pregnant," she says in a quiet submissive voice.

For a moment Jack's face lights up until he realises that this, apparently, is not good news.

"It isn't yours, Jack. I'm so very sorry."

The colour floods Jack's face, and then retreats to leave him ashen. He absorbs what he is being told. His own Frankie has been unfaithful to him. She is carrying another man's baby! How could she?

"Why? Who? I need the truth. Just give me the truth!"

Frankie sees his anger stirring, uncurling. Her tears stop. She owes him complete honesty.

"I didn't mean it to happen. It's just that you work such long hours and I was so lonely. That's not an excuse for doing what I did, but it's a fact. You and Anita were never around. You were always doing something else when we arranged to meet up. ..."

"Alex? Are you telling me that you are pregnant by Alex?" Jack is clearly shocked. Frankie cannot look him in the eye.

"Yes," she whispers.

"No! You are pregnant by your best friend's husband – my mate? How could you?"

"I'm sorry. I know how awful it is. I hate myself but you were never here, and Anita was always with the church minister, and we were both lonely, and well it just happened. We fell in love."

"How long? How long has this been going on?"

"About two years," Frankie is unable to bear the hurt in her husband's eyes. She looks down at the table.

"Two years! Hell, Frankie, you've been having an affair with Alex for two years? How can you live with yourself? More's to the point how could you live with me all that time knowing that you were betraying me?"

"I don't know, but I did, and somehow I felt justified. I believed you preferred to be at work than to be with Torrin and me. You could have told your parents that you needed to be at home more with your family."

"But you slept with Alex! I had to work; you know that!"

"Did you really have to work all those hours? I am so sorry, but you were hardly ever home and....don't you remember I begged you when Torrin was born."

Frankie sees Jack falter. His hurt and anger are all over his face, but she can tell her words have reached him. Perhaps he doesn't want to lose her even though she has betrayed him.

"Are you sure it's not mine?"

Frankie nods.

"Then maybe we can pretend it is. I can bring up the baby as my own child. I don't want to lose you." Jack is quietly weeping.

Jack hasn't cried since Torrin was born. Frankie hates herself. She stands and walks over to Jack. She pulls him to his feet so that she can hug him close. She doesn't love him, but he is a good man and doesn't deserve this.

"Can you really do that? I don't deserve you. If that's really what you want I will stay with you. I thought you'd throw me out."

The two stay in their embrace until Jack's tears dry up. They are both exhausted. They stand, clamped like two trees blown together by a storm.

"Does Anita know?" asks Jack.

"We agreed that Alex would tell her while I told you."

The telephone in the hallway starts to ring. Jack nods at Frankie as a sign that she should answer.

"It's me," Frankie immediately recognises Anita's voice. "Alex has told me. I understand why it happened. Maybe it's partly my fault. If you don't want the baby, I will have it, and Alex and I will bring it up together."

Frankie is appalled. "How could you even think that I would give up my own baby?" says the offended Frankie.

"Okay then. What does Jack say? Does he want it?"

"Do you think Jack would make me have an abortion, or that I would even consider agreeing to that?"

"Well, you couldn't blame him, could you?" comments Anita.

"No I couldn't. But I won't do that. Never." Frankie's voice is shaky now. "I'm very lucky. He wants to bring the baby up as his own."

"Okay. All sorted then." Anita hangs up. She had sounded completely unemotional about the whole thing. It's all a train wreck, Frankie thinks, but at least her baby was conceived in love.

That night Frankie slept beside her husband with her lover's child in her womb. Jack held her as she lay there in self-loathing. How they will all cope at church is another horrible thing to contemplate. Frankie shivers at the thought, wondering what life now holds for her.

— 23 —

Memory # 6 – Impossible to stay away

Frankie aged 27

"Frankie ... are you there?" It's his voice on the phone. "Hello? Frankie, it's Alex here."

Frankie knows that. She cannot find her voice. The sound of him brings it all back. Her love for Alex explodes from that compressed area of her heart where she has stowed it. For two months they have avoided each other in church and tried to ignore the fact that everyone is aware that something is wrong. The whole church knows that the two couples formerly so close are attempting friendship with other couples and spending less time together. Frankie and Jack and Anita and Alex cannot explain. Every morning Frankie has woken feeling deeply sad, longing for Alex but focusing on Torrin and Jack.

"Frankie ... are you there?"

She takes a deep breath. "Yes, I'm here. Why are you ringing?" Her pulse is pounding in her ears.

"I can't do it, Frankie. I can't stay away. I miss you too much. I love you too much ... I need to see you."

"What about Anita?"

"Anita won't even notice. She won't want to notice. She's only interested in church ministers. I've hardly seen her," Alex replies flatly.

"And Jack and Torrin? I haven't exactly looked happy for the past two months. They will notice if I start to see you."

"I know you're unhappy. I've seen your face at church and just wanted to come over and cuddle you. I think I'll just die if I don't have you somewhere in my life," comes Alex's broken voice.

"Do you think we can really manage it? You know I can't say No. I love you with all my heart and would do anything for us to get back together. The trouble is, if we do this, it will be much more difficult to keep it a secret than it ever was before."

"It will be worth it, Frankie. I can't live without you and it sounds like you feel the same. The past couple of months have been horrible, so what do you say? Will you meet me … please?"

Can Frankie resist her overwhelming need to spend time with the man she loves so deeply? Alex has made it very clear that they can never have a permanent life together.

"Hello. Are you still there?" Alex's voice sounds wonderful on the phone.

"Sorry. Yes I'm still here."

"So will you meet me?"

"Yes, I'll meet you," answers Frankie with a resigned but happy voice.

That evening Frankie thinks about the possible consequences of what she has just agreed to. Jack would not be so forgiving a second time. Torrin would be more confused about the situation than she already is if they were found out. Her parents wouldn't want her - that's for sure, and her grandmother is in a nursing home now so she would not be able to help. But Frankie really doesn't care. She has arranged to meet Alex in the morning outside the cemetery. He will be on his Vespa. The die is cast.

The next morning she is up bright and early, and after dropping Torrin at school, she parks her car in a side road and waits at the cemetery gate in excitement and anticipation. She can't calm her racing heart as Alex approaches on the yellow Vespa. He stops, passes her a crash helmet and she climbs on to the pillion seat.

"Is it safe for you to ride pillion?"

"I think so. I'm well over three months so it should be fine. Let's do it."

"Hold tight," says Alex as he pulls out into the traffic. Frankie hangs on. Excitement has returned to her life and she feels wonderful.

Half an hour later, they arrive at a woodland area and park the scooter in a layby. Frankie slides from the pillion seat, landing on a carpet of fallen leaves. She takes a deep breath of fresh air as she removes her crash helmet. Alex withdraws a small rolled up package from the box on the back of his Vespa. With crash helmets under their arms, Alex takes Frankie's hand and leads her into the dense trees and ferns. They move further into the woods until Alex is sure that they cannot be seen from the road. He places his crash helmet and package on the ground, and takes Frankie's helmet and places it beside his own. He pulls her close into his body and they embrace. It is not until Alex pulls away a little and starts to kiss her tears away from her flushed cheeks that she discovers she's been crying. Alex slaps his lips together saying, "Yum. Tasty tears."

Alex bends down to pick up the rolled up package.

"Tent," he explains as he rolls open the silky, coffee coloured package and together they erect the small, one-man shelter. Guy ropes secured, he unfastens the zip entrance, holds one flap open, and bows like a butler.

"After you, Milady."

Frankie giggles as she gets down on her knees and crawls inside. Alex follows and fastens the entrance zip. They lay on the ground sheet, cushioned by the soft woodland floor beneath, and slowly and sensuously undress bit by bit between increasingly passionate kisses.

Frankie feels Alex's touch, first on her breasts where he kisses and gently sucks both of her erect nipples; then on her almost flat stomach where he circles his soft kisses around her belly button; then down to her vagina where he strokes her with his tongue until she almost loses control. Meanwhile she has found his erect penis and begins to massage its hard length and lick its tip until he too is groaning with pleasure and need. At the very pinnacle of their yearning, he pulls her legs apart and both gasp as he gently but firmly pushes up into her as far as he can, touching the place that ignites Frankie into a frenzy of sensation and emotion. He pushes again as he kisses her deeply on her mouth. Every muscle in her starts to contract. He looks deep into her eyes as he pushes for a third time, her ecstasy being clearly visible in her blue eyes. He tries to control his urges as he rhythmically rocks back and forth, pressing again and again on that place deep within her that will take the woman he loves to the point of explosion. As her internal muscles clamp more and more onto his sliding penis, he knows he can hold back no longer. He climaxes with a groan as she follows with an orgasm that seems to go on forever. They cling together, fearing to let go in case the indescribable sensation that both are experiencing fades. The excitement gradually subsides, being replaced by a wave of emotion so strong that they know they have never loved each other as much as they do at this moment.

They lay beside each other in total lovely exhaustion. Frankie knows that Alex is truly the man of her dreams. For the very first time ever, she does not experience a flashback to the abuse of her childhood. They drift into a haze of sleepiness, holding each other's hand as they relax totally.

Over the coming months, Frankie and Alex make regular trips to the woodland. Even in the coldest part of the winter, they remain warm and cosy in their small tent, becoming increasingly efficient at rapid tent-erection. As Frankie's bump gets larger, their lovemaking necessarily gets gentler but no less passionate.

December arrives. Frankie is enjoying her Christmas preparations with Torrin. They make paper chains and decorations. They colour in Christmas cards, and make play dough models for the nativity scene. Torrin loves opening the doors of her advent calendar, and Frankie busily selects and packs the baby items she will need for her imminent hospital birth. She finds herself wanting to keep the house as clean as a new pin even though housework has never been her thing.

She finds it increasingly difficult to sleep, and one night she's particularly restless until, in the early hours of the morning, she suddenly feels a rush of warm fluid and knows that the baby is on its way. When she turns on the bedside lamp and throws back the quilt, to her horror she finds a large puddle of blood on the bottom sheet. Jack rushes downstairs to ring the hospital and they instruct him to bring her straight in. Within minutes he has thrown on his clothes, lifted the sleeping Torrin from her bed and onto the back seat of his car, and helped Frankie into the passenger seat. The roads are dark and empty and they reach Joanna and Frederick's house in less than ten minutes. Already alerted by Jack, Frankie's parents are ready to take the half-asleep Torrin from her parents.

Jack then drives at speed to the hospital, where the medical team is waiting for Frankie. A doctor sees her straight away, and wires her up to check the baby's condition. Even though Frankie is feeling no contractions, the doctor confirms that she is in labour, and the baby appears to be fine. Because of the bleeding the doctor takes her into the operating theatre to check if the placenta is in the baby's way. If it is, they will deliver the baby by caesarean section. Frankie is petrified. She shakes so much that her knees knock against the cold metal stirrups. To her relief, no emergency operation is needed, and within very few hours and with no pain, an eight and a half pound healthy boy is delivered. This time she instantly falls in love, as does Jack. The baby does look just like Alex but Frankie hopes that nobody else will see the likeness.

She feels energised when she and the baby boy arrive home in an ambulance a couple of hours later. Joanna and Torrin are waiting to welcome them. The new baby fascinates Torrin, but Frankie is concerned at how she will respond to the intrusion. Her daughter seems a little unsettled when she goes to bed that evening.

Each morning for the first week Joanna arrives to help look after Torrin while Frankie takes care of the new baby. After that, Frankie repossesses her home and her space, and takes the opportunity to ring Alex while Torrin is at school.

"I can't wait to meet my new son," says Alex. They arrange to meet at the cemetery an hour later. It is the week before Christmas and the weather is bitter cold as Frankie lifts the little boy out of his pram and into Alex's open arms. Alex looks decidedly uncomfortable, having never held such a small baby before. He seems relieved when Frankie puts the child back into his pram.

"Well done, Frankie," says Alex as he embraces her warmly.

"What will be his name?" she asks. "Jack is okay with Alexander if you want."

They have been considering either Charlie or Alexander for several months.

"Charlie would suit him, don't you think?" ponders Alex.

They separate after another embrace.

"Please take good care of yourself and our son, my darling, and have a happy Christmas." Alex disappears into the distance on his Vespa.

Frankie walks the baby to the school to pick up Torrin, who is proud to show off her new baby brother to her friends. Now it's only a matter of returning to church.

She feels disorientated and a little light-headed with fear as she walks into church on Christmas Eve with the baby in her arms and Torrin and Jack by her side. Frankie sees Alex in her son's every facial expression, and she can't believe that others won't see the likeness too. To her relief nobody seems to notice, but she wonders if the future will be as plain sailing as today.

— 24 —

Memory # 7 – Living a lie

Frankie aged 31

Charlie lets out a shrill scream. Frankie turns around in the passenger seat of the car to see Torrin with her hands over her ears and an innocent, wide-eyed expression on her face. Three-year old Charlie is strapped in his car seat next to his sister.

"Charlie, do stop that screaming!" Frankie pleads.

"Charlie is hurting my ears," exclaims Torrin.

"Did you do anything to make Charlie scream, Torrin?"

"No, I didn't do nufink."

"I didn't do anything – not nothing," corrects Frankie as she turns back to face the front. She has a strong suspicion that Torrin is not being truthful.

Torrin has found it increasingly difficult to tolerate her little brother and she takes every opportunity to distress Charlie, hoping that he will get blamed for the upset. Frankie suspects that her daughter pinches Charlie, but he never tells on his big sister. He seems to idolise her. He watches her every move and his love and pride for her shine from his eyes whenever she does something daring or dangerous.

Life jogs on for Frankie. In a strange way she feels that her little family is now complete. She loves to dress her son and daughter in identical style sweaters – one blue and one pink. She feels like she did when she was a child playing with her dollies.

She and Jack have become close friends with a different couple at church. Roy is a bit of a smooth talker and a church deacon like Alex. Roy's wife Julie is a rounded and homely sort of girl. Like Frankie and Jack, they have two children. The four enjoy going on day trips, and getting together on Saturday evenings.

Frankie now works part-time and, despite her feelings about her bullying mother-in-law, she allows her to take care of the two children. Frankie's job requires attendance at a training course some distance away one day a week. Roy gives Frankie a lift there and back, because he works near to the university where the course takes place.

The first time Frankie gets into Roy's car, he suggests that on the way home that evening they drop into a "Holiday Inn" for a drink. Frankie has no objection. Jack is collecting the children from his mum after work, and she would prefer to keep away from the woman. As agreed, they stop off and go into the bar, enjoy a quick drink, and then return to Roy's car. To Frankie's total surprise and dismay, Roy leans over to her seat and kisses her deeply on the lips, stroking her leg as he does so. She's speechless. She doesn't object or try to push him away and for some curious reason unbeknown to her self, she feels pressured to pretend she is enjoying it. Roy finishes the kiss, pulls away and turns the key in the car's ignition. Nothing is said for the remainder of the journey. Roy drops Frankie off outside her house and drives away. She goes indoors and carries on the evening as if nothing unusual has happened.

That night in bed, she cannot get the incident off her mind. 'How did that happen?' she asks herself. 'Why didn't I push him away and tell him to stop?' Those thoughts go round and round in her mind all night. She has no feelings for Roy, except liking him as a friend. Her deepest feelings are with Alex, and always will be. Roy and Julie's relationship seems solid, even though they often bicker, so Frankie really doesn't know why Roy thought it was okay to kiss her like that. She wonders if she is giving out inappropriate messages through what she says or does. Thinking over the car trip she can't come up with anything that might have encouraged him. Yes, she wears mini-dresses, and hasn't got bad legs, but that is just fashion. 'Maybe it was something I didn't do,' she thinks. 'Maybe if you say yes to a drink, that means you are saying yes to other things. But surely that can't be true can it? I'm either very naïve or there's something I'm missing here.'

Then finally, as she tosses and turns, a deeper question pops into her mind. 'Why didn't I push him away? Why did I just go along with it even though my whole being was saying 'No'?'

In the dead of night Frankie suddenly sees the link between the child sexual abuse she experienced and her inability to say 'No' to Roy. She learned to suppress her natural reactions when her father did what he did to her. She recalls the dilemma she felt at the time – the dilemma between knowing instinctively it was wrong and submitting to her father's authority because parents are supposed to know what's best for you. She remembers the deep need inside her to be loved and convincing herself that this was her father's way of proving he loved her. She remembers taking the bribes he offered knowing that she would then have to submit to his wishes.

Frankie suddenly understands herself. Roy gave her a lift. She owed him. She instinctively felt that he was entitled to take what he had earned. Just like her father took what he was owed. Frankie eventually falls asleep.

By the morning her moment of lucidity has disappeared, and has once more become entangled in the threads of her confusion just out of her reach. She speaks to Alex about it during one of their daily telephone conversations. He dismisses it as her misreading the situation. She decides to put it behind her and find an excuse not to stop for a drink if she gets a lift from Roy. This seems to work well until one Saturday evening when Roy and Julie come to dinner at Frankie and Jack's house.

Charlie and Torrin are in bed asleep by the time the visitors arrive. After dinner, Roy goes out to the kitchen with a bottle of vodka in hand, and is chatting with Jack as they do the washing up. Frankie and Julie chat in the lounge.

"What are you two girl's drinking?" calls Roy from the kitchen.

Frankie and Julie decide on lemonade and lime as they've drunk plenty of wine with their meal. The boys come in with a tray of drinks, turning the lights off as they do so. After handing out the drinks Jack sits next to Julie on one sofa and Roy sits next to Frankie on the other one. The girls are already quite tipsy so they don't even question why the boys turned off the lights. Slowly the chatting dwindles quite naturally. Frankie feels quite strange, very relaxed and floating in a happy haze. Roy pulls her onto his lap and starts to kiss her. Frankie is aware what is happening but feels no need to stop it. She thinks that Jack is kissing Julie too, but it doesn't feel in any way wrong. Roy slides his hand up the inside of her thigh and instantly Frankie is back in her childhood, sitting on her father's lap. Roy starts to caress her through her tights. It feels nice. The sensations she is feeling heighten in the way they did when her dad did the same thing. Frankie starts to argue with herself. 'This is wrong. This shouldn't be happening.' She forces herself to focus on the present. 'This is Roy. This is wrong.' She thinks about Jack doing the same to

Julie. She knows it is not something he'd do normally. 'What is happening? Why is it happening?' she wonders in her haze. She suddenly realises why Jack and Roy were in the kitchen for so long chatting. They were hatching a plan to swap wives for the evening. She can't believe it. Roy is a church deacon. Deacons don't think about doing such things. She doesn't connect what Deacon Roy is doing with what Deacon Alex does. She only knows that this is too out of character for Jack. She realises that the boys have spiked their drinks with vodka. Neither girl has ever drunk the hard stuff before. If Julie is feeling like Frankie feels, it is because of the vodka. Frankie summons up every ounce of her strength and slips off of Roy's lap saying,

"Okay you three. I'm tired and I need my sleep."

She gives Julie and Jack time to sort them selves out and turns the dimmer switch on to a low light. Roy and Julie stand up, thank Frankie and Jack for a lovely meal, and say their goodbyes.

Frankie clears up and goes to bed. A short time later, Jack follows her and switches off the bedroom light. Next morning Frankie's head is so painful that she can hardly lift it off the pillow. She learns what a hangover feels like.

"I think we had a bit too much to drink last night," says Jack as he slips out of bed and goes down to the kitchen to make coffee.

None of them ever discuss that evening again. After that, Frankie is very careful about what she drinks.

Later, Frankie tells Alex what happened. He is suitably shocked at Jack and Roy's behaviour, but she senses that he thinks she is exaggerating to make him jealous. She and Jack continue to socialise with Roy and Julie, but she makes sure that there is never an opportunity for them to engineer something like that again.

Time comes and goes until the spring of Charlie's fourth year. Every time Frankie goes to church she feels guilty and depressed. She becomes convinced that she can't continue to live a lie. She knows she will never be able to have a life with Alex, but at least if she leaves Jack and lives alone with the children, she will no longer be betraying Jack or the church. She thinks about it long and hard and knows this is something she needs to do. She has the income from her part-time job and decides that she will have to find a two-bed flat to rent in a cheap area, and claim benefits if she must, even though it is against her principles. She will then be able to continue seeing Alex without feeling the guilt that has been weighing her down for so long.

She doesn't relish the idea of the loneliness she is likely to experience if she makes this move. She has never before lived alone. She wonders how she will cope with the children. Will they rebel? Will they be unhappy without Jack around? Will they learn to live in a flat when they've become so used to living in a house with a garden? She would have to leave the church, all of her friends, and the children's friends, because the church believes in marriage for life. Even with all of these considerations, Frankie knows that she must leave Jack. She needs to say it out loud to somebody so that she can seal her contract with herself. Alex is the only one she can speak to. She knows that he will try to talk her out of it but she also knows that when he does, this will increase her determination. In her heart of hearts she believes that if you have a goal, you will always achieve it. Having made the decision, she rings Alex from the telephone in the hallway and runs her intentions past him, expecting him to argue her out of it.

"I'm coming with you," he says without a moment's hesitation.

Frankie is so shocked that she has to sit down on the bottom stair.

"What did you say?"

"I said I'm moving out and coming with you."

"What do you mean? You've always been very clear that you would never leave Anita or the church. You'd lose both. You don't have to do this just because I'm doing it. We can still see each other whenever you want to."

"Don't you want us to live together? Are you rejecting me?"

"Yes of course. I mean no I'm not rejecting you but yes I can't think of anything I'd rather do. But think about how it will affect the church. What about the young people that we both work with?"

"Frankie, I love you. I can't go on this way. The church will get over it, as will the young people. This is real life. We're young. It will be a long miserable life if we don't do something about the situation now. I want to wake up every morning with you beside me. I want to be with my son, and you know I've always loved Torrin. The children are young enough to accept change. Let's just do it!"

Frankie can't believe she's hearing this from Alex. Never once throughout all her heart searching, has Alex been part of the equation. She has always believed without question that he would never consider making such a move. This new idea starts to take shape in her mind. The move into loneliness and hardship has just become a move into joy and happiness. She knows it will require a huge amount of courage from both of them. Neither loves their partner but at the same time they have no wish to hurt them. Alex knows that Anita will be glad to see the back of him. She already spends as much time as she can with the new church minister. But Frankie knows that Jack loves her and the children and will be devastated.

"We need to start looking for somewhere," says Alex. "I'd prefer we get a mortgage and buy a flat rather than rent. Then when Anita and Jack are ready, they can sell the houses, give each of us our half of the money, and we can sell the flat and afford to buy a decent house with all the proceeds. They will then have their halves to buy somewhere else."

"I need to give Jack time to get used to the idea while I'm still here. He will need support. We will have to tell Charlie and Torrin – make it sound like an adventure so they don't get upset," Frankie replies, getting quite excited about the plans.

By the time they ring off, they have agreed to tell Jack and Anita as soon as possible. She wonders if she's dreaming. Can she really have a life of true happiness with the man of her dreams even though it will inflict so much unhappiness on others?

— 25 —

Taking stock

Frankie aged 50

Frankie opens her eyes. It's morning already. She's had a restless night, and feels very unsettled. As she lies in bed next to Alex, she tries to work out the reason for this. She's recalled several incidents from her past over the last two weeks, so why does she feel so unsettled? Then it comes to her.

'Good gracious. There are only two weeks left until my final meeting with my manager before I leave. I have to be ready to answer her questions at that meeting, and so far I haven't even thought about how the abuse affected my behaviour and how the counselling will change that. I need to take stock before any more memories come to my mind.'

Later in the day, she sits down with a notebook and pen, to recall the first memory. It was about meeting Jack and falling in love. She'd then fallen out of love but failed to end their relationship due to pressure from her parents, combined with feeling responsible for Jack's sadness. As a result they'd entered into what, for her, was an unhappy marriage. 'Why did I allow that to happen?' she reflects. She realises that as a child she'd succumbed to her father's pressure in the false hope that he would love her. Is that why she gave in to her parent's pressure to stay with Jack? Was she still hoping it would make them love her?

As Frankie thinks about this, she realises it rings true for her even now at the age of fifty. She still allows others to control her. She still sees herself as unworthy of other people's love, thinking that she has to earn it, and being surprised people like her even though she doesn't like herself.

Frankie heads her empty page 'How the abuse affected me' and begins her list:

1. Succumbs to the control of others
2. Feels undeserving of love
3. Feels unworthy of being liked
4. Doesn't like self

Frankie looks at her list and is shocked to discover how she feels about herself. She decides not to dwell on this discovery but to think about her second memory, which concerned her and Ralph, the Works Manager in the metal foundry where she'd worked. She was at a really low point when he came into her life, and they were drawn together by a common interest in her research projects. She knew Jack loved her, but she felt lonely and unloved because he put his parents and work before her. Ralph gave her the love and attention she needed. She realises that she didn't question his motives even when he disclosed to her that his wife was pregnant. Was he using her? 'Anyone with any self-respect would have walked away from him,' she says to herself.

Then she realises that was the problem. Her father hadn't respected her when he sexually abused her. Her mother hadn't respected her by colluding with the abuse. So how could she expect herself to have any concept of self-respect?

Does she respect and value herself now that she is a mature adult? The counsellor told her that the abuse was not her fault, but has that made any difference? She doesn't think it has. She needs to work on it. Maybe she should start to consciously believe that people like her for herself - just because she's likeable. That's something that has never occurred to Frankie before, and it sounds very inviting. She makes a mental note to correct every negative thought that she has about herself from now on. She finds herself feeling happy and excited at this prospect as she adds to her list:

5.   Has no self respect but aims to correct this

'Right, what did I remember next?' thinks Frankie in a more upbeat frame of mind. 'Oh yes, the time I realised I was pregnant with Torrin.'

She remembers how excited she was at being pregnant, and how she'd known it could be Ralph's baby, but would never be sure. Ralph certainly hadn't wanted to consider the possibility, and for the first time she wonders why she'd never questioned the man's motives – especially when he told her his wife was also pregnant.

'Maybe I felt that just presuming it was Jack's baby was simpler all round,' she concludes. She certainly hadn't thought through the implications for her child, and how it would cope with such shocking information if it ever came out? Even now, Frankie worries about the risk she took and is still taking. She realises how heavy the guilt still hangs over her, and how many times she has yearned to unload that secret to appease the guilt. 'How selfish that was of me,' she thinks, 'but what else could I do?' The alternatives might have broken up both her marriage and Ralph's, leaving her as a single mother. Jack's bullying mother would have ensured that it was all round the church in no time, and Jack would have suffered even more. Strangely, she recalls her father saying to her and her sisters when they were growing up, that if they ever got into trouble (meaning got pregnant), they could come to him. She feels sure his only form of help would have been to arrange an abortion and then wash his hands of it all.

'It's a pity I didn't understand the concept of risk assessment when I was that age,' thinks Frankie, wryly. 'Maybe I'd have either resisted the temptation to have an affair or at least thought about contraception. How odd that I wasn't too shy to have sex with Ralph but I was too shy to go into a chemist shop and ask for condoms.' She wonders why she had felt it was her responsibility to do that rather than Ralph's. 'Could it be true that he never loved me?' she wonders for the first time. 'Was he using me?' Frankie is shocked at the idea. 'Do I have to reframe my whole past life?' she wonders. That thought overwhelms Frankie. It feels like she is going to have to get to know herself all over again. She feels confused, and hopes her social work manager will be able to help her with that. Meanwhile she adds to her list:

6. Naïve?
7. Selfish?
8. Doesn't know self – needs help with this.

Frankie realises that taking stock of one's life is not a comfortable process. She doesn't relish the idea of making so many changes, but she is aware that if she doesn't, she risks making the same mistakes over and over again. She goes on to think about Torrin's birth – the intense pain, the lack of bonding, and the post-natal depression. Her mother, uncharacteristically, forced her to see the doctor, which surprised her at the time. Now she remembers the competition that existed between Jack's mother and her own, and feels that it was more than likely an act of one-upmanship to demonstrate Joanna's importance as Frankie's mother. But she also now wonders if her mother was showing some sort of love for the first time? That thought is enticing but she doubts if it's realistic, since her mother discontinued her regular morning visits after that.

Frankie now thinks about her problem bonding with Torrin. In hindsight she realises that being prevented from seeing her baby for so long was the probable cause of that difficulty. Added to this was the fact that the child looked a bit like Frederick. It was not surprising that this put her off from loving it immediately. She has always felt guilty for not falling in love with her own baby at first sight, but now the guilt lifts and she feels lighter as a result.

She remembers the day that Ralph came to call and how she rebuffed his advances for the sake of Torrin's future. She suddenly feels proud of herself. She'd made that decision on the day she left work and had stuck by it. 'That's got to be a positive for me,' she thinks, 'maybe I'm not as bad as I thought,'

This time she enjoys adding to her list:

9. Lack of bonding with baby not my fault
10. Stuck by my decision for the sake of Torrin
11. Stronger person than I thought

Frankie lingers on these last three points for a while, trying to boost her confidence and self-esteem, before she continues.

She feels proud that for three years after Torrin was born, she settled into a routine, and started to concentrate on her social life. She thinks fondly of the friendship with Anita and Alex, and how close they had all become. She feels ashamed that this culminated in her and Alex having an affair and her becoming pregnant. A second affair and a second pregnancy - a pattern was starting to emerge in her life yet she couldn't see it at the time. She wonders now how four practicing Christians could be so deluded. Anita was clearly still in love with the minister and not Alex, Frankie and Alex had fallen in love with each other and were having an affair, and Jack was oblivious of everything as a result of his mother's control.

'What a mess!' thinks Frankie. 'It's no wonder Torrin's behaviour was so bad.

She must have sensed all was not well and felt insecure.'

Frankie knows that circumstances threw her and Alex together, but she now realises that was not the cause of their affair. Adults should be capable of making responsible choices in their lives. She and Alex had chosen to have the affair. But that's not all. She was again having sex with another man and still not taking precautions to prevent pregnancy. Why hadn't she learned the first time? Was it that she thought she could get Alex for herself if she fell pregnant with his baby? She has no immediate recollection of consciously thinking that way, but she knows she will have to search her conscience to discover the answer to that question. She puts her list to one side for the day to give herself time to do that.

By the next morning, after a thorough conscience search, she decides that she'd just blocked the risk out of her mind. Clearly she doesn't learn from her mistakes, so the first thing she does is add to her list:

12. Choices (not circumstances) define a person's future
13. Failure to learn from previous mistakes
14. Taking responsibility for Torrin's behaviour

As Frankie re-reads the list, she realises she has a huge mountain to conquer if she is going to change her life for the better. She begins to understand that the counselling was not the end of her journey, but just the beginning.

She thinks now about the one thing that has remained constant - how much she still loves Alex. She recalls what a shock it was, when after two months apart, he had begged her to get back with him. She remembers the joy of their reunion, and later the birth of Charlie. She reflects on how relieved and happy she was to experience instant love for her tiny baby son. She also recalls how Jack had immediately bonded with the little boy, and then how relieved they were when nobody at church questioned his resemblance to Alex. 'So, what did I learn from that situation?' she wonders. 'I learnt what an amazing man Jack was. He not only stayed with me for the birth of another man's son but also bonded with that tiny boy and right from the start treated him as his own child.'

Frankie feels sad that she didn't love Jack. She wishes it had been possible to choose who she fell in love with, but concludes that if the chemistry isn't there, it won't happen. She adds just two points to her list:

15. Jack was a truly amazing man
16. If there's no chemistry, love won't happen

At this point, she thinks about the friends she and Jack made after they split with Anita and Alex. She liked Roy and Julie but still feels quite confused about Roy's behaviour. She understands why she hadn't rebuffed him when he kissed her in his car, linking it back to the abuse from her father, but she still can't believe what got into Jack when he and Roy spiked her and Julie's drinks with vodka in an attempt to have a wife-swapping evening. Perhaps Jack felt he needed more attention than she could give him. She recalls how she at least managed to bring that episode to a halt – another sign that despite all of her mistakes, she was still a strong woman.

Then had come the shock of Alex wanting them to move in together. Had she manipulated him? She is sure that wasn't the case. She'd just wanted to move away from Jack to ease her own guilt. Alex had always been quite clear that he would never leave Anita or the church, and she had believed him without question. Her next addition to the list was:

17. Life is unpredictable and full of surprises

Frankie takes a long last look at the list before she folds it in half and places it in her workbag ready for her meeting with her manager. She reflects on how useful an exercise that was, and wonders how many more points she will have to add to her list before the meeting. She feels apprehensive. Will there be more painful memories to consider?

— 26 —

Memory # 8 - Out with the old and in with the new

Frankie aged 32

Jack sits slumped on the sofa. Frankie sits beside him with her hand on his arm trying to comfort him.

"I'm sorry – I really am," Frankie says quietly, "I didn't know how else to tell you."

Jack starts to sob – big heaving sobs that come from somewhere so deep that his body trembles as they escape.

Frankie patiently waits for his sobs to subside before she continues.

"Jack, you are such a lovely man and you deserve someone much better than me. You know that I was pressured into getting married by my parents all those years ago. We've talked about it. Their only aim was to get rid of me, and any responsibility for me once and for all. I tried hard to split up with you way before we got married. I knew then that I no longer loved you in a romantic way. I failed because of the pressure they exerted on me, and I couldn't bear to see you so terribly upset. The last thing I wanted to do then was to hurt you. It's the same now. I just don't know how to avoid that any more. I love Alex. You've known that for some time, and yet you are such a kind person that you've brought up his son as your own. I can never thank you enough for that. I've watched you grow to love that little boy as much as you love Torrin."

"So in return you're going to leave my life totally empty by taking away the children?"

"Would you prefer I stay and continue to live a lie?"

"Yes!"

"I can't do it Jack. I'm sorry but I just can't. One day those children will grow up and leave home and what will we be left with? A loveless marriage and years more of unhappiness."

"I have enough love for both of us, Frankie. I can make you love me again like you once did. I can make you happy. How will all this affect Charlie and Torrin? Surely you can't do this to them just for your own selfish motives?"

"Charlie and Torrin are young enough to get over it. You can see them whenever you want. I have been unhappy all of my life. My father abused me with my mother's help, and then they forced me into a marriage that I always knew was wrong. I've tried to raise the kids with little or no knowledge of good parenting because I never had it, and through all of that I've done my best to be unselfish for the sake of everyone else because I thought that I wasn't worth enough to expect anything for myself. Alex has helped me to believe in myself again. I need to make this move for me. Now is my time."

Frankie knows that as Jack looks into her eyes, he sees there the determination he knows he cannot change. She has realised for a long time that it's her drive and passion that he has fed off, and she senses he is fearful of that being taken away. She also understands that he is frightened at the idea of going it alone. He's never had to do it before because his mother has always controlled him, even to the detriment of his marriage. Frankie senses that Jack now wishes he'd had the courage to stand up for her against his overbearing mother but it's too late and she hopes he realises why it has come to this.

"Okay, Frankie, you win," he says in a resigned voice. "I suppose I always knew we'd get to this point some time. I know I haven't been what you've needed. I'm weak and I'm sorry I've let my mother bully you so often, and I haven't been around when you've needed me. I have to take some of the blame for letting things go this far. Thank you for caring enough to give me time to adjust to the idea before it happens. Alex is a good man and I know he will love Torrin as much as I love Charlie."

With that, Jack leaves the room and goes upstairs to bed. Frankie finds some pillows and blankets in the airing cupboard, and makes up a bed for herself on one of their two-seater settees. Despite her legs hanging over the arm of the settee, she sleeps better than she has done for many months.

At seven the next morning, she opens her eyes to the sound of her eight-year-old daughter and four-year-old son racing each other downstairs. They rush into the lounge and stop dead when they see their mummy laying in her makeshift bed. They ask no questions, but instead jump on top of her, taking the opportunity to have a three-way pillow fight, giggling each time their aim hits the mark. Frankie plays along for a while, and then stops the two over-excited children, calming them down for breakfast. It's a school day and Torrin is already wearing her school uniform, whilst Charlie is dressed ready for his half-day in the nursery class. Frankie has a busy day ahead of her. She's made an appointment for her and Alex to speak to the mortgage broker. Today marks their first step towards a new life of love and happiness. She can't wait to get started.

They quickly secure a mortgage and the flat search begins. A week or so later, the new church minister knocks on Frankie's door. She isn't surprised. She's been waiting for him to call, assuming that Anita probably already told him about the plans she and Alex have. As they sit chatting, she opens up her heart to him about her and Alex's love for each other. To her surprise, the minister encourages her to go ahead. She is stunned, having always believed that the church would not only frown on it, but also do its best to stop it happening, as the Reverend Jones had. Things must have moved on in the Baptist movement without her realising it.

Frankie soon finds an ideal flat and puts in an offer, which is accepted. The owners are part of an on-going chain of purchasers, so there is a long wait to acquire their home. Surprisingly Jack quickly comes to terms with the situation and starts to date other women. But he gradually hardens towards Frankie. One evening while they are discussing her pending departure, he gives vent to his anger and lashes out, hitting Frankie with such force that she falls to the floor. One of her eyes and her cheek swell up and she's badly shaken. Jack immediately expresses regret for what he did, but Frankie, though shocked and in pain, feels relieved that he's given vent to his feelings. In a strange way, it's a relief to her to be punished. She knows she deserves it, and when people enquire, she explains away her black eye and swollen face as being the result of her clumsiness in not looking where she was going. She tells them she walked into the edge of a half open door.

A few days later, Frankie and Alex are looking after the children while Jack is out on a date. The time has come for them to tell Torrin and Charlie about their plans. Frankie is nervous, but she knows she must be honest and clear. She is worried about how her daughter will take it. The child idolises Jack, as he does her.

"Torrin, we need to talk to you, please," says Frankie at the end of a game of "Ludo". Alex pulls Charlie on to his lap. Frankie holds Torrin's hands.

"You've probably noticed that Daddy and I haven't been spending much time together lately," Frankie begins, "In fact we've been spending more time with Uncle Alex than Daddy."

Torrin's face is serious as she nods her head.

"That's because Daddy and I don't love each other like we used to," Frankie continues.

Torrin bursts into tears. Frankie pulls her onto her lap, holding her close. Charlie sits quiet and still, clearly not understanding what's going on.

"Why are you crying, Torrin?" Frankie asks gently.

"Because you don't love Daddy anymore," sobs her daughter.

Frankie realises that she's underestimated her eight-year-old daughter's understanding of love, and feels clumsy and incompetent at not even being able to tell her daughter in the way the child needs.

"I'm sorry, Torrin. I didn't want to make you cry. It's just that sometimes grown-ups' feelings change and they stop loving a person. Daddy and I still love each other as friends, just not in the way we need to if we are married." Torrin quietens down enough for Frankie to continue. "The thing is, Uncle Alex and I have come to love each other in the way that makes us want to get married."

"So will we all live together – you, Uncle Alex, Daddy, Charlie and me?" pipes up Torrin.

"No, darling. Daddy will live here, and we will live in a different place. It will be like an adventure. We will live in a flat with lots of other families around us. You will have new friends to play with in the big garden."

"But won't Daddy be lonely living all alone. Won't he miss us?"

"No, Daddy will be fine. He's out making lots of new friends right now," reassures Frankie.

"And you will be able to visit Daddy whenever you wish," adds Alex.

"Will Daddy stop loving me and Charlie when he's made his new friends?"

"Torrin, your Daddy will never stop loving you," says Alex, "and you are lucky, because instead of only having one daddy who loves you, you'll have two."

"Will I have two as well?" asks Charlie whom everyone has temporarily forgotten. Alex hugs Charlie. Torrin looks wary.

"Yes, you'll have two just like Torrin," confirms Frankie, smiling and tweaking her son's tight, strawberry blond curls as he shrugs her off. It's time for bed, so Frankie takes Torrin by the hand and Alex carries Charlie on his back as they ascend the stairs together. Each have a bedtime story and a kiss goodnight, but when Alex tries to kiss Torrin, she turns her head away.

One week later, just a week before Christmas and with snow on the ground, the re-formed family moves into its new home. They have very little in the way of furniture and carpets – just bunk beds for the children, a double bed for Frankie and Alex, and a carpet and two chairs in the lounge. What they lack in material belongings, they make up for in happiness and love.

Torrin and Charlie each desperately want a bicycle for Christmas. Frankie and Alex manage to scrape enough money together to grant their wishes even though finances are very tight. The children appear shocked and surprised to discover what Santa has left them when they wake up on Christmas morning. Torrin confesses that they had secretly feared that the big man might not have realised they've moved away from their old home.

After that, life settles down. The divorces are set in motion, and the children start their new school, where they fit in very quickly. Frankie works hard to make ends meet and eventually suggests to Alex that they speak to Jack and Anita about selling the two houses. During that conversation she discovers that Alex has been paying a substantial amount of maintenance to Anita, who gave up her job on purpose when he left.

"How could you do that when you know I've been struggling to feed us?" she asks angrily, realising this is their first disagreement.

After a short and harsh exchange of views, Alex confesses.

"I felt guilty because I inflicted the situation on Anita and she did nothing to deserve it."

"You put your ex-wife before me and the children," comes Frankie's retort, "while Anita gives up her job and lives like a queen. Do you think we deserve that, Alex?" Frankie storms off, wondering if all men are weak.

Both Jack and Anita respond positively to the letters they receive from Frankie and Alex. Jack informs Frankie that he's getting married to a girl he met after she left, and who is now living at their house. Anita explains that she and the new church minister are doing the same. Frankie realises now why the minister gave her the surprising advice he did.

Frankie's divorce moves slowly because Jack refuses to share the furniture from the house. Frankie and Alex desperately need a dining room table and some bed linen. They have no money to buy these items. After many attempts to negotiate, the solicitor advises Frankie to go to the house when nobody is there, and take the items she is entitled to, which she does.

The following day, Frankie answers a knock at the door, but before she can get it properly open, the visitor, who turns out to be Jack's fiancée, slams into it and punches Frankie hard on the face. Frankie reels backwards from the blow as the woman walks away without a word. The attack brings back memories of the day Jack lost his temper and hit her. She knows she deserved that, but definitely not this. Alex comes rushing to Frankie's aid, holding her close until she stops trembling, then applying a cold compress to her swollen and bleeding face. They are both astounded and mystified as to the woman's motive, but grateful that the children didn't witness the incident. Frankie thinks that violence has followed her, in one form or another, all her life. First her father Frederick, then even Jack hit her, and now his stupid fiancée has beaten her.

They decide not to involve the police in what has already become a very acrimonious situation, and after much wrangling with Jack, his solicitor and the bank, the finances are sorted out, Frankie and Alex sell the flat, and the family moves into a new house.

Torrin and Charlie react badly to the move to yet another new school. Torrin becomes more rebellious, and Charlie becomes very introverted and unemotional. Frankie and Alex hope that they will gradually settle down. The divorces come through. Frankie and Alex get married with Torrin as bridesmaid and Charlie as pageboy. Within a few months, Frankie is pregnant and eventually gives birth to a little girl who they name Adele. Frankie wonders how Torrin and Charlie will react to a new little sister after all of the other changes they've had to accept.

— 27 —

Memory # 9 - Enough is enough!

Frankie aged 38

"Hello. Can you help me? My fifteen-year-old daughter hasn't come home."

Frankie has been pacing the floor since Torrin failed to arrive home at 10.30 p.m., her school-night curfew. Alex has been in bed since eleven. It's now one o'clock in the morning, and so she has rung the police.

"Okay, Madam. We'll take a few details and radio a couple of our beat officers to look for her," says the police operator.

Torrin has become increasingly rebellious since Frankie, Alex and the children moved to their new house when she was ten years old. She settled down for a while after her new little sister, Adele, was born three years ago. She was charmed by the baby and spent many hours helping to take care of her. She seemed happier than she'd been for a long time, but over the last six months things have deteriorated and now gone from bad to worse. Whatever Frankie has tried by way of disciplining Torrin, it's failed. She knows Torrin is displaying typical teenage behaviour in that she is rude, disobedient, and whatever she's asks or tells her to do, she does the opposite. Frankie has sought advice from family, friends and professionals. She and Alex have attended films, and read books on good parenting, but nothing works. All they have learned is that their child is at the extreme end of defiance, probably because she is highly intelligent and is not being stretched at school. Frankie and Alex have spoken to the school about their daughter's behaviour, but they strongly suspect that the school values Torrin as a talented table-tennis player, and would rather have her as part of the team than discipline her for failing to do her homework or bunking off. Frankie is at her wits' end.

Frankie has now woken Alex and they are sitting together in the lounge hoping that their daughter hasn't come to any harm. The two beat officers, one male and one female, knocked half an hour ago to get a better description of Torrin, and to gather some information about where she usually 'hangs out'. They also asked for permission to give Torrin a harsh warning when they bring her home. Frankie and Alex agreed, gaining some comfort from the fact that the officers were clearly assuming that Torrin wasn't hurt.

Now it's a waiting game. Frankie can see Alex's frustration is building. He has a responsible job looking after the information technology department at the local college. She knows that this requires all of his concentration, and sleep deprivation makes life difficult for him. Both are deep in thought, wondering what they have done wrong with their eldest daughter when there is a loud knock on the front door. They instantly snap out of their reverie and, with hearts thumping, they race to open the door.

"Hello again, Sir, Madam," says one of the officers.

Standing between them is Torrin. Her fiery eyes fall first on her mother and then her stepfather.

"Come in," says Frankie, opening the door wider.

All five walk into the lounge.

"We found your daughter not far from here in an alley behind some houses. She was with a group of youngsters," explains the policeman.

Torrin doesn't look in any way sorry or ashamed of herself.

"Haven't you got anything to say to your parents, Young Lady?" the officer continues. "They have been worried sick about you."

Everyone focuses on Torrin, who remains silent.

"Okay. Then just listen because I have something to say to you," he says sternly.

Frankie squirms at the tone of his voice but Torrin turns her belligerent stare on him and holds eye contact as he speaks.

"You appear to have no respect or concern for your parents – in fact you seem to go out of your way to make life miserable for them. They care about you and love you or they wouldn't have called us tonight. The only thing you show in return is defiance and disrespect verging on cruelty. You are the sort of young person that ends up getting into bad trouble, or worse, getting injured. If you don't want to end up in prison or hospital, I suggest you open your eyes and see just how lucky you are to have a caring and loving family. Many kids of your age aren't in that position and maybe you couldn't blame them for going off the rails, but you come from a good family, have a lovely home, and clearly have some intelligence. My advice to you is to take a long look at yourself and consider your future. I could take you to the police station for an official warning for wasting police time, but this time I will just leave you to think about what I've said!"

Frankie instinctively wants to berate the officer for talking to her child in that manner, but she knows that Torrin needs to hear his words if she is to be stopped from continuing on her path to self-destruction. Torrin continues to stand on the same spot, and displays no emotion. Frankie thanks the police officers and shows them to the door. The female officer touches her on the arm sympathetically before she leaves. That sympathetic touch brings tears to Frankie's eyes and threatens to take away the control she is trying so hard to exercise. She takes a deep breath, pulls herself together and returns to the lounge just as Torrin turns around and heads for the lounge door, purposely hitting against Frankie's arm as she passes, and saying in a quiet but haughty voice,

"Who do they think they are!"

Frankie tries to hold Alex back as he instantly reacts to his stepdaughter's words, rushing after Torrin and grabbing her arm.

"How dare you, you arrogant little madam. You've put your mother through hell and you are going to apologise to her!"

Torrin looks squarely at him and from between gritted teeth says, "Who says so?"

Frankie can hardly watch as she hears her husband's response.

"I say so!"

"Oh yeah. You're not even my real father, so how are you going to make me?"

Frankie knows where this is going. The usually placid Alex has passed the point of no return. He grabs Torrin and gives her a thorough thrashing. She is powerless to stop him. He has become Frederick and she has become her fifteen-year-old self. She freezes in horror. She knows that Torrin deserves to be punished, but not like this. Then she sees Alex come to his senses and move back from his stepdaughter with a look of horror on his face. Torrin rushes past, thumps upstairs loudly and slams her bedroom door hard behind her. Frankie hears a whimper from Adele but then all goes silent.

She knows that her eldest daughter is probably comforting the little sister she loves very much.

Frankie looks at Alex who is standing with a dazed expression on his face. She puts her arms around him and he holds her tight as he whispers,

"I'm sorry. I'm so, so sorry!"

"Okay, darling, it's okay. Try to calm down. I can feel your heart beating so just try to take some deep breaths or you'll end up having a heart attack."

"I lost it, Frankie, I lost control. I let my anger take me over. I couldn't stop myself. I'm so very sorry!"

"It's alright, Alex. I know how Torrin can wind us up. I too was very angry, and she did deserve to be punished."

"I need to say sorry to her, Frankie. I need her to know I shouldn't have hit her."

"Let's just leave it for the moment, Darling, it's so late and we are all very tired. Speak to her tomorrow when we've all had some sleep and she's calmed down."

Alex lets Frankie lead him upstairs and they both fall into bed exhausted, Frankie once more wondering how it is that violence seems to follow her like a slow and intermittent wave.

The next morning after Charlie has left for school, and Adele is playing happily with some toys on the lounge floor, Alex insists on going up to Torrin who is still in bed. Frankie accompanies him. Her daughter is tucked up under her quilt with her eyes closed. She has become such an attractive young woman. Looking at her now, Frankie can hardly believe how badly behaved she is. She gently touches her child's shoulder.

"Torrin, wake up please. Alex wants to speak to you."

The teenager's eyes open but she says nothing. She doesn't look at Alex as he speaks.

"Torrin, I want to apologise for losing my temper last night. What you did was and still is unacceptable, but the way I dealt with it was also unacceptable. I'm sorry for hitting you. I can only say that mum and I were tired and worried and I lost it. It won't happen again, but I hope you will think about what that police officer said to you."

Torrin turns over to face away from her parents, but says nothing. Alex and Frankie leave the room.

Things don't improve. Torrin's behaviour gets worse. Frankie is so stressed that she dreads the sound of her daughter's key in the lock, knowing that it heralds a palpable increase in tension. Then it comes to a head.

Torrin reaches the age of sixteen. She has completed her GCSE exams at school and left. She didn't do well in the exams, despite being a highly intelligent young woman, and she hasn't attempted to get a job. She spends her days sleeping, only rising mid afternoon to get ready to go out clubbing. She rarely has contact with Jack, who contracted multiple sclerosis a couple of years ago, and she only rings him when she wants money, which he invariably hands over. Frankie has spoken to Jack on the telephone and asked him to consider not acquiescing to Torrin's every request. Torrin has a boyfriend and comes and goes as she wishes, flouting all rules and attempts to control her behaviour. One afternoon Frankie confronts her daughter who is standing in front of the mirror in her bedroom applying her makeup.

"Torrin, this can't go on," she begins, "You are making the whole family's life hell. You need to be in by a reasonable time at night so that we can at least get a good night's sleep without worrying about you. You also need to get a job so you can start to contribute to your keep."

The belligerent teenager completely ignores her mother and carries on with what she's doing.

"Are you listening to me, Torrin?" comes Frankie's raised voice.

"I'll do whatever I wish," declares the girl, not looking at her mother when she speaks. Frankie takes hold of Torrin's arm and turns her daughter to face her.

"You will listen to me, Young Lady," she says assertively.

Torrin lifts her free arm and hits her mother hard on her face, sending her reeling backwards. Frankie is silenced for an instant, stunned that violence has once again erupted, and when she speaks, it sounds like the growl of an angry bear.

"That's enough, Torrin, you will get out of this house right now. You've overstepped the mark and I will not have you here ruining the lives of the rest of us. Get out now!"

Somehow Frankie finds the strength to drag her daughter downstairs, and push her out of the front door. She then locks both the front and back doors before she collapses onto the lounge sofa. She hears her daughter banging on the front door and window shouting to be let in. She ignores her. Torrin then goes around to the back of the house and through the garden, and does the same. Frankie is aware that all the neighbours can hear the commotion, but she also knows that for her own sanity she cannot let the girl back in. One more moment of stress will be one moment too much. She knows that she is at breaking point and can take no more. She buries her head in her hands to shut out the noise and sits paralysed to the spot.

Eventually Torrin stamps off and peace returns. Frankie takes a deep breath. She realises that right now she doesn't care where her daughter goes. She knows she ought to care but somehow she is devoid of any emotion at all other than a deep sense of relief. She wonders what will happen now.

— 28 —

Memory # 10 - The premonition

Frankie aged 39

"Hello. I'm Torrin's boyfriend's mum. I just wanted to let you know that she is safe and currently staying here with us. I didn't want you to worry."

"Oh that's really kind of you to let me know," responds Frankie, holding the phone to her ear. "Thank you so much. Are you okay with her being there?"

"Yes. I'm sure everything will settle down in a few days, and she is welcome to stay here till then."

"Thank you. I can't tell you how grateful I am. Thank you again for ringing me. Bye."

"Bye."

Frankie is relieved to hear that Torrin is safe, but the thought of her returning home in a few days still feels unpalatable. Her daughter has been away from the house for a day and Frankie is still feeling only relief.

The next few days are blissful for her. Family life feels good without the tension. She can breathe deeply again. Charlie and Adele are easy to manage, although Frankie suspects that her youngest daughter misses Torrin badly. Alex is less edgy and spends time giving Charlie and Adele his attention.

After a few days, Frankie is ready to have her daughter back home again. The respite has given her renewed energy and determination to be a good parent to all three of her children. So when she hears Torrin's key in the door, she finds herself looking forward to seeing her eldest daughter. She goes into the hallway to greet her in the hope that she can give her a hug and both can agree to move forward in a more positive way. Her daughter is about to go upstairs when Frankie reaches her.

"Hello, Torrin. It's nice to have you back. I just wanted to say …"

"Before you go any further, I'm not staying. I'm just getting some things," says Torrin in her usual sullen voice.

"What do you mean? Are you going back to stay at your boyfriend's house?"

"No. A guy I know who owns a house up the road has said I can stay there," responds Torrin with a victorious tone in her voice.

"What guy?" asks Frankie.

"You don't know him. He's a friend from the pub," sneers the sixteen-year-old.

Frankie is taken aback. The thought of her tension-free days lasting a little longer is an inviting prospect, but the thought of her daughter living in the house of a stranger who she has got to know in a pub is not.

"Who is this man? What are you doing in a pub at your age? Where is his house?"

Frankie can hear herself getting more and more panicky. So much for her determination to make things different! She knows she is coming over as the heavy parent.

"Number 42 up the hill and on the opposite side of the road," replies Torrin dismissively as she continues to walk upstairs and disappears into her bedroom, closing the door quietly behind her.

Frankie can't think straight. Why would this man invite her daughter to stay at his house? Does he just feel sorry for her or has he got a different agenda? Is her daughter putting herself in danger? Does she understand the risks? Then Frankie chastises herself. 'Just a few days ago, you threw your own daughter out without even a thought for where she would go or what danger you might have put her in. You, Frankie, are one big hypocrite!'

Guilt and regret flood her. All she wants to do is protect her eldest daughter and keep her safe, but she has no idea how she can prevent the determined Torrin from starting on this road to possible danger. She hears the bedroom door opening and closing, and her daughter descends with a full rucksack, passing her mother on route to the front door.

"Torrin, please don't go. I'm worried for your safety," she says quietly.

Her daughter doesn't look at Frankie but silently carries on to the front door, opens it and quietly closes it behind her.

Frankie feels only confusion as she stares at the closed front door.

"Where has Torrin gone, Mummy?" Adele has come out of the lounge where she was playing.

"She has decided to live in a house up the road, Darling. No need to worry. I expect she'll pop in to see you whenever she can," explains Frankie, trying to sound calm for the sake of her five-year-old daughter. Adele seems satisfied with this explanation and disappears back into the lounge to continue her game.

When Alex gets home from work and hears what has happened, his concern is obvious, but he tries to reassure Frankie.

"It might be the best thing for Torrin right now, and maybe it will help her to gain a sense of responsibility for herself, and also a sense of gratitude for what she has here at home," he says. Frankie nods hopefully.

Over the next few days, Adele repeatedly asks when her sister is coming home. Frankie becomes increasingly concerned, so one day while Charlie and Adele are at school, she walks up the road and knocks on number 42. After a short pause, Torrin opens the door. She says nothing but turns around, walks a short way up the hall, and disappears through a door on the left. Frankie enters, and closing the front door behind her, she follows her daughter. She finds herself in a dowdy lounge, where Torrin has laid herself down on a grubby brown sofa. Her face is shockingly pale. She looks to have lost a significant amount of weight.

"Are you unwell?" asks Frankie tentatively.

"Yes," responds Torrin sulkily.

"What's wrong?" asks Frankie.

"I just feel ill," says Torrin.

"Will you come back home, Torrin?" Frankie tries not to sound as if she's pleading.

"No."

"Have you been eating?"

"Yes."

"Where are you getting the food?"

"I take what I want from the kitchen."

"Please come home, Torrin, so I can take care of you," pleads Frankie, no longer caring about hiding her desperation.

"No."

"Will you let me arrange for the doctor to come and see you?"

"Okay."

"Thank you. I'll go back home and ring him now, and then come back and tell you when he will be coming."

Torrin gives a barely visible nod, before Frankie disappears out of Number 42 and walks as fast as she can down the hill and back home. She rings the doctor's surgery and arranges a home visit for that same afternoon, saying she will meet the doctor there. She returns to her daughter and tells her the time of the home visit, saying she will come to be with Torrin when he arrives.

"I don't want you with me," declares Torrin in a voice that doesn't leave itself open to questioning.

Frankie is disappointed but nods and says goodbye to her clearly unwell but still belligerent daughter, knowing that she won't be able to settle to anything until she knows what's wrong with Torrin. She watches out of the front window and sees the doctor drive up the hill at the allotted time. She runs after him to explain that her daughter will not let her be present during the consultation. He is a kind and gentle man, and squeezes Frankie's arm before he rings the doorbell. Frankie walks away but glances round to see Torrin open the door and let him in. She waits for him to leave before she returns to ask what he said was wrong with her. Torrin's only response to her mother's question is, "Nothing."

"Torrin, please come home. Adele is missing you badly, as we all are. Let's forget that all of this ever happened and start afresh," she pleads, looking straight into her daughter's blank eyes.

Torrin shakes her head and turns over to face the back of the settee. Frankie stands still for a moment before she gives up and returns home feeling sad and discouraged.

She hears nothing more from Torrin for several days. She knocks at the door of Number 42 time after time but there is no response. Then she bumps into one of Torrin's friends who tells her that Torrin has moved in with another friend in a different town and is believed to be working for a minicab company in the same area. The girl has no contact details for Torrin so Frankie has no choice but to give up. But she is relieved to hear that her daughter is working and wonders if

Alex's prediction of her learning to take responsibility for her self has come true.

After three months they still haven't heard from Torrin. Frankie thinks about her every day, but she tries to stop worrying by working hard. She feels sad for Adele who cannot understand why her big sister hasn't come to see her, but she also feels more and more relaxed without the stress that she has lived under for so long. Then one afternoon, Frankie starts to feel very anxious. She has a premonition that something is wrong with her eldest daughter. She tries to disregard it, but the feeling gets stronger and stronger until she can ignore it no longer. She remembers the town where Torrin's friend said she was staying, and she also remembers that she was working for a cab company. After dinner Frankie sits down and begins to trawl through the telephone book. There are over fifty minicab companies in that town. She goes through her list, ringing each one in turn and asking if Torrin works there. After a couple of hours, during which she becomes increasingly discouraged, she eventually hits gold. The lady at the other end of the telephone confirms that Torrin works for the company and promises that she will get her to ring Frankie when she comes on duty later in the evening. Frankie feels very relieved that not only has she found her daughter, but that she is also okay. She waits patiently for the telephone call but it hasn't come by midnight and she can't stay awake any longer. She goes to bed and soon falls asleep.

It feels like she has only just closed her eyes when the telephone rings.

It's the lady at the cab company that she spoke to last night.

"Sorry to ring so early but I'm just going off shift and I didn't want to keep you hanging for another whole day." Frankie glances at the clock. It's 6 a.m.

"That's okay. Thank you for ringing me."

Frankie's heart is thumping with anticipation and hope.

"Bad news I'm afraid. Torrin didn't come in to work last night and we've no idea why."

"Oh," Frankie responds, unable to prevent the obvious disappointment in her voice.

"I'm so sorry it's not the news you were hoping for. If I hear anything, then I'll let you know."

"Thank you. I'm so grateful for you taking the time to ring me. Bye."

Frankie puts the receiver back in place gently, and creeps back upstairs, sliding in beside Alex. She feels devastated. The premonition that something is wrong stays with her, but she has to learn to live with it because the cab company doesn't ring her back. Nor does her eldest daughter.

— 29 —

The Final memory - Betrayed

Frankie aged 43

"To the man I love most in the world at the moment."

Frankie has moved on from her part-time job and has been working as the manager of an older people's day centre for almost three years now. It's the first day of an annual holiday she arranges for her clients. Alex always accompanies her on these holidays, and is now off playing snooker with the husband of one of her staff members.

Frankie re-reads the words on the card she has just found near the top of Alex's rucksack while looking for the camera. It's what she expected but dreaded to find. For two years she has suspected that Alex has been having an affair.

It's something she has discussed with her sister Janet, who told her that Alex loves her too much to even contemplate such a thing. Frankie chose to put it to the back of her mind in the hope that it would go away. After all, why would Alex have an affair?

"He loves you too much to do that, Frankie, you can see it in his eyes," Janet had said. Charlie and Adele are staying with Janet while Frankie and Alex are on this holiday.

Frankie reads the card again. As the truth finally sinks in, it hits her like a hard punch in the stomach. It winds her, and her head starts to swim. She sits on the edge of the bed to recover. She knows immediately who wrote those words. Her name is Lara, a pretty woman with soft blond curls who's married to a policeman named John. She was Charlie's first schoolteacher. When Lara moved on to work in the college where Alex works, Alex took her out to lunch as a welcome, something that Frankie thought was a great idea. Then Lara started to place her students for work experience at Frankie's day centre, which meant they had fairly regular contact. Frankie had always liked Lara, but her sixth sense came into play, warning her that Lara could not be trusted completely.

Alex's behaviour started to change. He started to pick fights for no real reason, and on several occasions she caught him glancing at her with a disdainful expression on his face. She was hurt and confused and didn't understand why. Alex started to work late more often and even though she felt lonely, she accepted his reasons. Charlie was now sixteen, and Frankie enjoyed the extra hours she had with him at home.

Frankie became really worried when Alex stopped showing his affection, and was no longer interested in making love. Then she knew for certain that all was not well. But she still chose to ignore it. Until today. Frankie now knows what she must do. She walks over to the reception area of the holiday camp they are in, goes into a telephone booth and rings Lara.

"Hello Lara. Are you going to tell John you are having an affair with my husband or shall I?"

There is silence at the other end of the phone. Then Lara says quietly, "No, I'll tell him."

"Good, and from now on you'll stay away from Alex or I'll make life at the college very difficult for you."

"Okay," responds Lara. Frankie replaces the receiver. Her hand is shaking. With the offending card in hand and feeling as if she is operating on remote control, she walks to the snooker room where Alex is mid game.

"We need to speak right now," she interrupts.

Alex doesn't argue. He places the snooker cue on the table and follows her out, leaving his playing partner looking shocked. Back in their chalet both sit down. Alex obviously knows something is wrong.

"Do you love Lara?" asks Frankie with heart thumping.

"Ah. You know. Yes, but that doesn't mean I don't still love you," responds Alex.

"Do you intend to leave me and the children?"

"I don't know."

Frankie is shocked. He is the man of her dreams and even though he says he still loves her, he's considering leaving her. He gave up everything to be with her, and now he is willing to do the same to her as he did to Anita. He has a son and small daughter who he adores, and he's considering walking away from them too. Frankie can't believe it. Her self-loathing surfaces as she convinces herself that she isn't worth Alex's love, but she refuses to accept he can walk out on Charlie and Adele.

"I need to know everything, Alex. I can't deal with what I don't know so please don't keep anything back."

As Alex starts to tell all, Frankie knows she will do anything to keep him. She loves him too much to lose him. It occurs to her that she is now finding out how Jack must have felt when she told him about Alex. Poetic justice, she thinks.

As she listens to the details and asks questions, which Alex appears to answer truthfully, her anger is slowly replaced with deep shock and sadness. She can't understand what she has done to make Alex look for love elsewhere. Is she too needy? Does she ask for too much reassurance of his love all the time? She realises that she has always thought that Lara was a bit on the prowl, probably because her husband worked such long hours and she was likely quite lonely, but why did she have to pick on Alex? Then she remembers she was the same when Jack was always at work, and in fact that's why she and Alex got together in the first place. But she thinks about the happiness she has had with Alex and needs to understand why it obviously wasn't the same for him.

'Maybe it's the tension from not knowing where Torrin is. It's obviously had an effect on me, and maybe he has needed to look elsewhere,' she thinks. As she questions and listens, she decides that would be understandable, and she can't blame him for finding it all too much. Then the sadness overwhelms her and she sobs deeply, unable to stop her self. Alex makes no attempt to comfort her. She feels intensely bereft.

As she starts to calm down she manages to speak. "I need to go home," she tells Alex. I just need us to have a night on our own to come to terms with this."

Alex agrees, so she puts her deputy manager in charge, and without a thought for her lack of professional responsibility, drives home like a woman possessed. She vents her anger through her driving speed, and feels better for it, especially when she notes Alex's white knuckles as he hangs on to the edge of his seat.

They discuss the issue most of the night until they fall asleep through sheer fatigue. The next morning they agree that Alex will ring the minister of the church they now attend. She hears him confessing to the man over the phone. It all sounds so cheap compared to the love they've shared together.

When they return to the holiday camp a day later Frankie finds herself following Alex around like a little dog. She can't let him out of her sight. She uses all her energy to disguise the hurt inside her from her colleagues and clients.

She is mentally and physically exhausted by the end of the holiday.

After that she finds she can't return to work. It's as if the shock has paralysed her. She spends hour after hour sitting in the lounge looking into space. Alex and the children seem to come and go in the daze that has become her daily existence. One day she looks over at the low cabinet on which sits the music system. She suddenly knows there is something important behind it. Her sixth sense is telling her. She brushes the system onto the floor without a thought, and pulls the cabinet away from the wall. Behind it she finds a receipt for a pair of earrings that aren't hers.

She waits for Alex to come home and then insists that he contacts Lara to tell her to return the earrings to him now. An hour later Lara and John arrive in their car. Frankie asks Lara the same question she'd asked Alex, "Do you love him?" When Lara says she does but has decided to stay with John, Frankie's anger overflows. How arrogant of this woman to hurt Alex so much! She can't quite believe she feels angry on her husband's behalf rather than for herself but she does, and she attacks her husband's lover in the front garden in full view of the neighbours. Alex and John have to pull her off and Lara is very shaken. Frankie feels better that she's inflicted humiliation and hurt on the woman that hurt them both so much.

Alex confirms that he won't leave Frankie and with a huge sense of relief, she returns to work. She tries to make everything appear normal for the sake of Charlie and Adele. She finds this hard to maintain and on one occasion when the anger inside her boils over she removes Alex's beloved guitar from the bottom of the bedroom wardrobe and jumps up and down on it until it is smashed into pieces. Charlie walks past the bedroom door just as she is venting her anger and looks shocked.

"Okay if I go out, Mum?" he asks in a quiet voice.

Frankie readily agrees, wishing her son hadn't witnessed the incident, and then proceeds to cut Alex's favourite jumper in half. She feels better for giving him a taste of the hurt he caused her.

For a long time, new questions come up about the affair, and Alex tries to answer them as best he can. After several months, things get a little easier as time seems to heal. Gradually the questions get less, until Frankie realises she has forgiven him. She knows, however, that she will never forget the hurt he caused her, and will never be able to truly trust Alex, or indeed any other man, again.

— 30 —

The Final meeting

Frankie aged 50

"You came to bed late last night."

Alex is making breakfast in the kitchen when Frankie appears dressed and ready for work. She sits beside him at the breakfast bar.

Adele, now sixteen, the only one of their three children still living at home, is upstairs in her bedroom studying for her exams. Torrin eventually got back in touch not long after Frankie's attempts to find her through the mini-cab company. Frankie's premonition proved correct. Torrin had suffered some bad experiences, but she returned home and fully recovered from them. She is now not only beautiful but has become a sensible young woman of twenty-seven, living in her own flat and enjoying a very active social life. Charlie joined the army at sixteen and at twenty-three is stationed in the Midlands, so is only able to come home from time to time.

"Yes, sorry Darling, I was finishing my list for my final meeting with my manager today," explains Frankie. "I can't believe that this is my last day on placement. I'm really going to miss the other team members."

"Do you think you've passed?" Alex asks.

"I really hope so. It's been such an amazing journey, what with my counselling after I almost lost it with that elderly man when his daughter disclosed he'd sexually abused her and her sister as children, and then that young man in my team dying so suddenly. I've also learned so much. I just hope I can put it into practice in the future."

"I'm proud of you, and so should your manager be," encourages Alex as he slips on his jacket ready for his walk across the park to the college. "You're a very clever woman, you know." He kisses Frankie goodbye.

"Bye, Adele!" he shouts up the stairs as he passes.

Then all is quiet. Frankie takes a last sip of tea before she, too, shouts goodbye to her daughter and leaves the house.

When she enters the team office for the last time, her colleagues look up and smile.

"How you feeling, Frankie?" asks the team clerk. "Your last day working here."

"Sad," replies Frankie. "I'm going to miss you lot."

She makes a coffee and busies herself tying up loose ends, completing her case notes, and making a few telephone calls before her manager calls her in to the office.

"So here we are. It's the last day and just a couple of questions left to answer from our last meeting," says the manager as she passes Frankie another coffee.

Frankie gets out her list of learning points, and starts to go through it, explaining her reasoning as she goes. She highlights that she's learned about the need to like herself if she wants others to like her; and her tendency to submit to the control of others even though she's a stronger person than she'd previously given herself credit for.

Then they arrive at the memory about the ending of her first marriage and the beginning of her new life with Alex.

"What did you learn from that episode?" questions her superior.

197

"For one thing, it consolidated the fact that my parenting skills were still lacking. I completely underestimated Torrin's reaction to hearing that I no longer loved Jack."

"It took courage to make that final break for the sake of your own happiness, though. Clearly your self-esteem had improved a little by then, and to some degree you had recognised that you deserved to be loved."

"That's true. As I said earlier, I have worked out that if I don't like myself, I'm never going to be able to believe that others like me."

"And the fact is, others do like you, Frankie. I can vouch for that."

"Thank you. Knowing that fact increases my confidence, and that makes it easier to chat with people than it used to be. It especially helps when I'm engaging with new clients. I think that they trust me more easily if they see that I'm confident."

Frankie then remembers all the problems she had with Torrin. "Of course, I made a right mess of things by kicking Torrin out of the house when she was only sixteen. I feel so ashamed of that, but at the same time I realise that the way I reacted was again due to my lack of parenting skills. I'd never learned them from my parents so I just didn't know what else to do."

"You said earlier that you tend to give in to the control of others because you were so controlled by your father. Think about it. Wasn't Torrin trying to control you? It seems to me that for the first time ever you were resisting that control. Is that not a positive thing? Perhaps you shouldn't be so hard on yourself," suggests the manager. "After all, from what you've told me, she's grown up to be a very sensible young woman so you must have done something right."

"That's true, and in a way, wanting to strangle that old man was probably a good thing. When I felt that, I was resisting his ability to control his wife and abuse his daughters. If I'd just ignored what his daughters had told me; I think that would have amounted to being controlled by him."

"Believe me, there are lots of controlling people out there, including some of the clients we work with. I can't see you being controlled by anyone in the future. I think that you will always do what's right. After all, you said earlier that you'd discovered you're a strong woman," reminds the manager. "You even stuck by your decision to discontinue that first affair for the sake of your daughter, and that shows that you're not selfish too."

"I think the counselling has made a real difference to me. Just knowing that none of the abuse I experienced was my fault has taken away so much guilt. It has helped me to like myself more, and to understand why I behave in certain ways. Knowing why will help me to change my behaviour. So not only have I discovered that I'm a strong person, but I've also realised that I can empathise with people who've had similar experiences to me. Armed with this new understanding of myself, I believe I'll make a more effective social worker. I'm determined to turn all my negative experiences around and use them in a positive way to help others."

"Frankie, you have shown during your time with us that you have a natural empathy for others. You are kind and caring and have a lot of love to give. Yes, you were a little naïve in your younger days, and maybe inadvertently selfish here and there, but that was not your fault - just the result of your childhood experiences. You have shown me that you are willing to accept responsibility for your own actions, just as you did when you decided that Torrin's behaviour was down to you. You have strong values and clearly want to do what's best for others, and you've demonstrated that fact during your placement with us. Your approach has been intelligent and professional and you have shown a willingness to reflect on situations and learn from them even when the process is painful for you. You did that during your counselling and again today by answering the questions I gave you last month. Also, if and when things go wrong, you are willing to work hard to put them right. You did that after Alex had that affair, and you did it after your inappropriate reaction to your client's husband. I want you to know that you have gained the respect of everyone in the team, which should encourage you to have greater respect for yourself. Well done, Frankie. You've passed your social work placement with flying colours."

Frankie's eyes light up on hearing the news she was hoping for. Her manager comes around her desk and gives her a big hug before she says with a grin, "You've got a great bum too!"

Frankie laughs out loud as she opens the office door. The others see her smile, but they already knew the news was good.

"Three cheers for Frankie! Hip hip hooray, hip hip hooray, hip hip hooray!" All her teammates are standing in a group. Party poppers go off. A champagne cork explodes, flies across the room and hits the ceiling. One of her colleagues pours the bubbly into glasses and passes them around. As Frankie accepts her glass, the team moves apart, and she sees that her desk is covered in colourful parcels and greeting cards. She can't hold back her tears of happiness and gratitude any longer.

"Speech! Speech!" shout some of the members of the team.

Frankie blows her nose, takes a deep breath and begins ...

"I can't tell you how touched I am, not only by your generous gifts but also by your generosity in accepting me into your team, sharing your knowledge with me, and helping and supporting me during my time with you. I've learned so much both about social work practice and about myself. Now I need to put everything I've learned into passing my final exams, getting my qualification, and being the best social worker I can be. I hope I'll be a credit to all of you. I'll keep you up to date with my progress because since you made me so welcome, I've decided that once a member of the Learning Disabilities Team, always a member of the Learning Disabilities Team. Don't think you're getting rid of me that easily. I'll be back regularly to see you all."

A few cheers and faux groans erupt at this statement.

"Finally I want to say that although this is the end of my placement, it's also the start of my new life. I need to make personal changes as I move forward. My pledge to all of you is that I'm going to turn all the negative experiences of my childhood into positive help for others. One of the things I've learned is that life is unpredictable and full of surprises. I have no idea what trials and tribulations may come my way, or how I'll overcome them, but now I know my own weaknesses, I'm determined to gain victory over them. So wish me luck, my lovely friends, as I face the future head on. Wish me success as I work to make a difference to the lives of other. And once again, thank you all."

"To Frankie's future!" says the team manager raising her glass, "May her weaknesses become strengths and her negatives become positives!"

The End

Maybe the future seems impossible
But you can find it.
The fog will lift
The strength will come
Your feet will walk towards tomorrow
And then, one day, you will find
That you have lived your way into it

Janet Doyle, an Australian writer
based in Central Victoria, 2018

Author Biography

Gloria Eveleigh

Gloria Eveleigh was a research metallurgist before a career change to social work. She designed and led the first local authority multi-agency framework facilitating the safety of vulnerable people. She has run a safeguarding consultancy and worked across the UK setting up community groups and training volunteers to support the recovery of victims of abuse.

The mother of three grown up children and five grandchildren, Gloria lives on the south coast of England, writing, and chairing her local Parish Council. She has written and illustrated 24 phonics-focused picture storybooks for small children.

In the 1940s and 50s, when child abuse was hidden, not believed, and not acknowledged, Gloria had first-hand experience of growing up in a dysfunctional family. She and her three siblings were the victims of familial physical and sexual abuse.

In this autobiographical novel Gloria is now happy to tell her personal story. She hopes that it will help others who suffered childhood abuse, or who are currently experiencing abuse, to believe in themselves, to know they are not alone, and to know for sure that there is hope of recovery. Her aim is also to give professionals working with victims a greater insight into the short and long-term effects of abuse on those who experience it.

CPSIA information can be obtained
at www.ICGtesting.com
Printed in the USA
BVHW041543220819
556561BV00016B/3424/P

9 781643 671581